My

Miraculous

Moments

Gail H. Johnsen

My Miraculous Moments
By Gail H. Johnsen

For permissions, information about book orders, or to contact the author, go to:

gailhjohnsen@gmail.com

Book Categories: LDS, Faith

Book Cover by Liz Bartlett Rolfson

Published by Gail H. Johnsen

First Edition, April 2016

ISBN 978-0-692-47170-8

Dedication

This book is dedicated to my husband, Gary, and to my children, Stuart, Clark, Guy, Clayton, Jocelyn, Zane, and Karen, who are important ingredients in *My Miraculous Moments*. I would also like to dedicate it to my extended family: my sisters, Jan H. Duffin and Juliet Emmer, and also my brothers-in-law, nieces, and nephews. They have taught me so much just by being part of my life.

A special thank you to my niece, Dr. Janalee Emmer. Her help as both editor and encourager during the writing of my early stories, and later her assistance and advice helped me to complete this work.

I also want to acknowledge my friends who shared many of these miraculous moments with me, and also all the members of the church in the various locations where I have lived who are part of many of these stories.

Gail H. Johnsen

Proceeds from
My Miraculous Moments
will be given to
Primary Children's Hospital
in Salt Lake City, Utah

Table of Contents

Preface

In 1990 I began publishing my stories in periodicals of The Church of Jesus Christ of Latter-day Saints. I was grateful for the favorable responses I received from friends and family. Later, I decided to gather these stories and others that had occurred in my life. I did this not because I think they are unique, but because it is my desire that something I learned might be of value to others. I also hope they will strengthen the reader's testimony as they have mine.

I believe that all of us have miraculous moments, and I trust that my stories will allow others to recognize and remember the miracles they enjoy in their own lives. I hope that we will see the importance of writing and recording our personal experiences for the benefit of others, especially our family and our posterity. Our written testimonies of the restored gospel of Jesus Christ are a loving legacy we can leave behind when we are gone.

It is my prayer that each of our memorialized miraculous moments may create a body of evidence that build unshakable testimonies in us and in our families. Like Jacob in the Book of Mormon, I hope we may be able to say that, "Notwithstanding the many revelations and the many things which I had seen concerning these things; for I truly had seen angels, and they had ministered unto me. And also, I had heard the voice of the Lord speaking unto me in very word, from time to time; wherefore, I could not be shaken" (Jacob 7:5).

Part of my motivation for compiling these stories came from a list of questions posed by the late Truman G. Madsen, who was an emeritus Professor of Philosophy at Brigham Young University. In his book *Five Classics*, the author explains that he received a phone call from a young man who wanted to know if Brother Madsen still had a testimony of the gospel after receiving his Ph.D. in Philosophy and Religion. Brother Madsen sought to understand the basis for this question and invited the caller to meet with him. Shortly after their discussion began, it was clear that his visitor did not really possess a testimony of the gospel. Brother Madsen decided to ask him twenty questions to explore what his experience had been in the church. Those questions are as follows:

Prayer:
1. "Have you ever prayed and been lifted beyond yourself, both in the manner and in the content of your expression, so that it became more than a dialogue with yourself?"

The Sacrament:
2. "Have you ever had the experience of feeling the wounds on your soul being soothed, being filled with the Spirit that warms, and thus being quickened in a hunger and a thirst to return to the sacrament table where you find healing?"

3. "Has it been as if you were taking hold of a couple of electrodes and were subject to a current?"

A Patriarchal Blessing:
4. "Have you ever had the 'thin veil' experience? When a patriarch made promises to you, declaring your heritage

and something of the promise of your destiny, was it as if you were surrounded by glorious, but somehow less tangible, persons?"

The Scriptures:
5. "Have you had the 'before and after' experience of Joseph Smith, who speaks of reading the scriptures after receiving the gift of the Holy Ghost?"

6. "Are there times when the scriptures leap off the page and bomb you, hit you between the eyes and as it were, between the ribs such that you know these phrases were written under inspiration and you see clearly how they apply to you?"

Ordination:
7. "Have you ever, in receiving the priesthood, or an office within it, or a calling to serve felt 'liquid fire' or what the Prophet himself spoke about as 'virtue' which somehow passed from the person into you?"

An Instrument:
8. "Have you ever been involved at the other end, *being an instrument* for setting apart or ordaining or baptizing or confirming? The Savior said, 'Ye shall have power that to him upon whom ye shall lay hands ye shall give the Holy Ghost' (Moroni 2:2). Have you ever had the experience of thus being a vehicle?"

Testimony:
9. "Have you ever stood up because there was an almost compulsive lift to stand? Did you have the sensation of being, as it were, outside yourself, listening to yourself,

when your words came with a transparent clarity, running ahead of your ordinary thinking; and you felt the core of your soul coming to the fore with a glow of unqualified conviction?"

10. "What about others who have spoken in your hearing? Has there never been a case...when you have listened to the 'living oracles' at the head of the Church, when you were sure the person was speaking beyond his natural ability, when *the power of his testimony* seemed to cut through the fog and go directly to you?"

Beyond Natural Ability:
11. "Have you ever been able to speak or act beyond your own natural ability?"

Spiritual Gifts:
12. "Have you ever had such gifts, that are mentioned in Moroni 10, Doctrine and Covenants section 46, or 1 Corinthians 12, especially in serving others?"

13. "Have you sensed, say, the gift of discernment—the gift of the word of truth or knowledge—or the gift to teach it, or of wisdom or the gift to teach that?"

Pure Intelligence:
14. "Have you ever received what the Prophet calls 'pure intelligence flowing into you,' or a quickening in your soul that binds you to a truth or a person or a sacred place; a power toward something or away from something that you cannot trace into your ordinary environment? Or have you just known by the spirit of prophecy that a certain thing was going to happen? I am not talking about wishes,

guesses, hopes or hunches; I am talking about the phenomenon of *just knowing*?"

Music:
15. "Have you ever sung a hymn, or is there a single piece of music in this Church that speaks to your soul in a way that others do not?"

Conscience:
16. "Have you ever been guided by your conscience with a clear 'No?' Or, have you had your conscience 'gnaw(s) at us' as the Prophet put it?"

The Temple:
17. "Have you felt anything about the promise given at Kirtland referring to the House of God as a 'place of holiness?' Are you constrained to acknowledge as you enter the temple, that it indeed is 'a house of glory, a house of order, a house of God' (D&C 88:119)? Have you had the feeling or the sense of the sacred?"

Love:
18. "Do you find that you have the kind of love like the Savior's so that you are able to see others deeply, but seeing them, you are able to overlook the things that would otherwise antagonize you?"

3 Nephi 17:
19. "Do you respond with anything unusual in reading Third Nephi?"

The Testimony of Jesus:

20. "Have you received the 'testimony of Jesus?' Is the most thrilling prospect of your life not simply to imitate Jesus in behavior patterns, but *to become like him* in nature, in very attribute and appearance, and eventually, even though being begotten of him with all that means, *possessed of his power*?"

Brother Madsen records that he could probably answer yes to at least 18 of them. The young man however answered "no" to seventeen questions, "maybe" to two, and "yes" to one. Brother Madsen then suggested to his young friend that he hadn't really been in the church. When this statement offended his visitor, Brother Madsen explained, "No, the church's flowing powers have not really been in you whatever the location of your Sunday afternoons."[1]

These twenty questions caused me to mentally evaluate my own experiences, and then to begin recording them more carefully in my prayer journal. That process of accumulating and writing these personal events resulted in the stories that I share in this book.

---

[1] Truman G. Madsen, *Five Classics* (Salt Lake City, Utah: Eagle Gate Publishing, 2001), 148-161. (Used by permission)

A frigid and snowy Salt Lake City morning welcomed me on January 16, 1950. It was exactly mid-month and mid-century. Although the world may not have been very inviting on that damp and dreary day, it ushered me into a planet filled with both miracles and misery, rich in life and learning. I have been blessed to recognize that they each have their purpose and to appreciate them equally.

When Dr. Skidmore delivered me and told my dad about the new arrival my father's response was, "Another girl?" I was the fourth child in the family following first a boy, Patrick, and then two other girls, my sisters, Jan and Julie. When I was two years old, Patrick was accidentally killed by a friend while they played cowboys and Indians with my father's loaded gun. He lived two days after he was shot, then died in a Salt Lake City hospital. While I was too young to remember all the details of this incident, it had a major impact on my family. A few years later my parents adopted my aunt's baby, Frank.

Shortly after that our family moved from Salt Lake. We lived in both North and South Dakota, and finally settled in Blackfoot, Idaho when my father purchased a family shoe store. That was an important day for my parents, and living in Blackfoot had a significant influence on me as I grew up. After high school, my friends and I attended Ricks College (BYU-Idaho) and then we all went to Brigham Young University.

When I turned 21 I decided to interrupt my college studies to serve a mission. I was called to the California

North Mission, headquartered in Sacramento. When I returned to BYU, I finished my degree with a B.A. in Speech and Drama, a minor in English, and a secondary teaching degree. I also became better acquainted with my husband, Gary Johnsen, who served in that same mission. During our married life, we have lived in Westwood, California; Gillette, Wyoming; Carlinville, Illinois; Spring, Texas; the U.S. territory of Guam; and Draper, Utah. In 2011 we served a senior mission together in Micronesia Guam and were located in the Republic of Palau.

As I mentally survey all these events of my life, one stands out. I was baptized in the old tabernacle in Blackfoot when I was eight years old. Little did I realize then that a battle would ensue for possession of my soul. I have often been surprised by both the intensity at which the adversary, Satan, tries to lead me away from my covenants, and the tremendous amount of help I receive every day from my Heavenly Father that enables me to hold onto the iron rod. These gifts are given to all of us through the restored gospel of Jesus Christ, the constant companionship of the Holy Ghost, and the example of the Savior's life.

My Miraculous Moments contains some of my favorite experiences which have both bolstered my testimony and blessed my life. I am grateful for the privilege of sharing them.

Baby Birthmark

When I was born, I had no outstanding visual disfigurements, but I did have a tiny birthmark under my chin. It was a dark, cherry red dot, and even though it was small, it would have grown as I grew and spread over my face. Because I was naturally a little shy, I believe an unusual facial feature would have made a huge difference in my life. My mother asked her doctor if anything could be done to remove it. He explained that there was a new treatment for the removal of this kind of blemish, and my mother agreed to this innovation. My best recollection is that they used some kind of dry ice remedy, and after each treatment I had a little pus bag hanging from my chin. It took three sessions to fully remove it, each 6 months apart, but they ended while I was still a toddler.

Throughout my life, I have had a small scar there, but I have always felt like it was a miracle in my life. Although the procedure was new at the time, it worked. My Heavenly Father, a watchful mother, and a very good doctor were able to prevent this potential trial in my life. As I have pondered this event over the course of many years, it has confirmed to me that my miraculous moments began very early in life. The words to Sally Deford's Song, "He Is There" come into my mind when I think of this corrected childhood defect. Here are some of the lyrics:

He is there
When the first uncertain breath of life is taken
He is with us when our mortal souls awaken
So unaware

He is there
Close beside us in each moment we are given
There to light our way, and lead us home to heaven
He is there

He is there with love beyond our understanding
Watching o'er us with a Father's tender care
With all His might and mercy never-ending
He is there[2]

A scripture in the Pearl of Great Price punctuates this principle so exquisitely. Enoch inquired of the Lord, "How is it that thou canst weep, seeing thou art holy, and from all eternity to all eternity?" Then he continues with these insights about the Lord, "And were it possible that man could number the particles of the earth, yea, millions of earths like this, it would not be a beginning to the number of thy creations; and thy curtains are stretched out still; and yet *thou art there*, and thy bosom is there; and also thou are just; thou art merciful and kind forever" (Moses 7:29-30, italic added by author).

Although I have not been spared every difficulty that life has to offer, I was protected in this instance while I was still a little child. I have come to believe that when I stand before my Father in Heaven to account for my life, I will

[2] See Sally DeFord, "He Is There," http://www.defordmusic.com/sheet-music/alphabetical-list/he-is-there/

fall on my knees in gratitude for the blessings of healing and protection like the one I had as a baby. I also believe that I will praise His name for the restraint it must take to allow me to suffer for my choices, and also to be able to learn from experiences that try my soul. What a Perfect Parent we have! He is always there watching over us, but He knows what we need to learn, and also what we promised to do while we are on the earth. If I have learned anything in this life, it is that our Father in Heaven is truly there.

The Big Bible

When I was young, my mother took us to church every Sunday, even though my father was not involved in any way. I didn't always want to go to church, but I knew my mother felt strongly about it because she told me that I was going, and that she would take me in my pajamas if I didn't get dressed. I believed her! Once I got to church though, I loved hearing the lessons and was always irritated when the other children were noisy.

I know something now that I didn't know then: my mother had a strong testimony of the gospel. She knew that the church would have a positive influence on my life, and that living its principles would save me from many problems.

My mother's parents were both members of the church and sealed in the temple, but the death of a beloved first child and other cares of the world worked on their testimonies, and they were not always committed to living the gospel. Because of this, my mother started drinking and eventually smoking, and then married my father who was also a member of the church, but not active. It took her many years and some miracles of her own to overcome her earlier choices, and she didn't want us to have those addictions. My mother eventually served two missions— one to the Swiss Temple and a proselyting mission in Portland, Oregon.

Besides what I learned and felt at church, I remember one occasion when I was playing down in the unfinished basement of my friend. I found a large Bible and because we were a little bored, I sat down on a bed that was set up in the family room and plopped that book on my lap. I was in elementary school, either first or second grade. While I holding that Bible I felt something warm and very real. I started talking to my friend about one of the scriptures I knew, and in essence bore a testimony to her. The feeling became even warmer and stronger when I spoke.

I believe it was a witness from the Spirit about the importance of the divine written word that we have been given, and an example of the way Heavenly Father works with children. He wants us to know how it feels to be in His presence and to have the gift the Holy Ghost.

The scriptures have sometimes been called true scripts. "Script" brings to mind one of the tools of the acting trade: the written words and direction for a play or a performance. When we memorize these phrases and perform them, we try to become the person that we are portraying.

The scriptures are like performance materials that teach us how to become more like the Savior and our Heavenly Father, but they are *true* scripts. If we follow them correctly, we can literally take on the character of the Father and the Son. This is accomplished as we study the Holy Scriptures, memorize them, and become what we read. The Holy Ghost encourages us to not only read and study the scriptures, but also helps us to understand how to use what we have learned.

I believe that I received a witness from the Spirit at a very early age that the true scripts that I held in my hands would direct my life and show me how to live it. We are promised that, "Angels speak by the power of the Holy Ghost; wherefore, they speak the words of Christ. Wherefore, I said unto you, feast upon the words of Christ;

for behold, the words of Christ will tell you all things what ye should do" (2 Nephi 32:3). These words from Elder Dallin H. Oaks make me even more determined to be diligent in my gospel study: "The scriptures can also help us obtain answers to highly specific personal questions."[3] I testify that to the extent that I use them in my life, I have had increased direction and help.

In addition to the miracle that the scriptures are in our lives, I have learned that there is power in just having them to hold. The Family Home Evening Resource Book suggests: "Let children have their own scriptures. Get each child an inexpensive set of scriptures, even though they are too young to read. They will love to have their own books, and you can help them mark some of the stories you read. As they learn to read, help them ahead of time with scripture assignments so that they can read them during family home evening. Older children and teenagers often enjoy being able to explain terms or give background information for assigned scriptures. Be prepared to help with these assignments, to offer suggestions and sources of information."[4]

The prophet Isaiah understood the impact gospel knowledge would have on children when he said, "And all thy children shall be taught of the Lord; and great shall be the peace of thy children" (Isaiah 54:13). What better blessing can we give our children, our families, and ourselves than peace? I know that this priceless gift of

[3] Dallin H. Oaks, *Scripture Study—the Power of the Word Teacher Manual*, rev. ed. (Church Educational System manual,2001), 45.
[4] *Family Home Evening Resource Book* (Salt Lake City, Utah: The Church of Jesus Christ of Latter-day Saints, 1997), 167.

peace in my life comes when I live the lessons that I have learned from the scriptures.

My love of the standard works began at a very early age and has continued as my testimony has strengthened and as I have been given further light and understanding through the true scripts that the Lord has provided the world.

Fanning My Fledgling Faith

The first time I remember receiving a real answer to prayer came when I was about 12 or 13 years old. Entering the teen years caused me to pay more attention at church, and I tried harder to understand what I was being taught. I wanted to have my own testimony that the gospel was true, and I also wondered if it would make a difference in my life. I started praying for some specific blessings, and it felt like my requests were not getting past the ceiling.

My mother had a powerful testimony of prayer, but I didn't really know that until I told her about my feelings on the subject. She encouraged me to keep praying. She promised that the Lord would hear me.

It was shortly after this that I specifically asked the Lord to help me refrain from arguing with my two siblings—my older sister, Julie, and my younger brother, Frank. We were the only children living at home at the time. I don't remember why I was bothered by the arguments. Perhaps I had heard something in my Primary classes, or in Sacrament meeting. The disagreements weren't horrendous or even huge shouting matches, but suddenly I didn't feel happy about them.

Not long after these particular prayer requests were made, I began to see that whenever a verbal conflict would begin I became ridiculously tongue-tied. I was in the midst of "a war of words" as Joseph Smith expressed in his personal history, and suddenly I would be verbalizing absurdities. This always stopped the fighting and caused me and my siblings to laugh.

These interruptions in arguing are among my earliest memories of getting a direct answer to my prayers. I learned that even though I didn't always know for sure if I was truly able to access heaven with my petitions, the Lord did listen to the earnest prayer of a young woman.

I love the poem entitled, "Prayer":

> I know not by what methods rare
> But this I know, God answers prayer.
> I know that He has given His word
> Which tells me prayer is always heard,
> And will be answered, soon or late.
> And so I pray, and calmly wait.
> I know not if the blessing sought
> Will come in just the way I thought;
> But leave my prayers with Him alone,
> Whose will is wiser than my own,
> Assured that He will grant my quest,
> Or send some answer far more blest.[5]

Learning at a young age that my prayers were both heard and answered created a foundation of faith and trust that has continued throughout my life. It became easier for me to pour out my whole soul to the Lord because I had begun to believe in the power of prayer. The more I prayed, the stronger my evidence of the efficacy of the effort. It has sustained me through every trial, challenge, and question that has confronted me and been the source of many miracles.

---

[5] Eliza M. Hickok "Prayer," *Best Loved Religious Poems*, ed. James Gilchrist Lawson (New York: Fleming H. Revell Company, 1933), 160.

The Lord Is My Light

Growing up in a small town in Idaho proved to be very
advantageous for me because I was always surrounded by
committed members of the church who taught me the
gospel and who demonstrated how to live it.[6] It was
particularly helpful because my father, who was a member
but not actively participating, lived in a way that could
have influenced my choices. This was especially true as a
teenager when the decisions I made became more crucial in
determining the course my life would follow.

Our family had always lived in town, but when we
moved out to the country where there weren't any street
lights, I found that the roads were somewhat scary after
sunset. I wouldn't have ventured very far outside at night
with a friend, much less by myself. I was afraid of the dark.

One serene summer evening, I found myself alone at
home finishing the dinner dishes and cleaning up the
kitchen. While working, I opened the refrigerator and saw a
bottle of alcohol on the shelf. I also knew that a drawer
nearby held some cigarettes. In our home, there were
family members who didn't live the Word of Wisdom, but
it was never a temptation to me. I had no desire to try either
of them and had never considered either smoking or
drinking before.

After I completed my tasks, I climbed up on the kitchen
counter to relax for a few minutes. Suddenly, the thought

---

[6] See original publication: Gail H. Johnsen, "The Lord is My Light,"
Deseret News, August 6, 2015.

came into my mind that I could smoke one of the cigarettes and drink some of the alcohol. This idea was very confusing to me. It was followed by, "You are alone. No one will ever know."

Instead of persuading me, the thought that I was alone had the opposite effect. I felt sure someone else was there. This someone wanted me to break my promises to Heavenly Father and was hoping to entice me away from the things I knew were right.

I became frightened but remembered that I could pray and receive help, direction, and the companionship of the Holy Ghost. I bowed my head and said a silent prayer. After that, I knew I needed to hop down from that counter and get out of the house. Like the story of Joseph in the Old Testament, I felt I needed to flee from temptation (Genesis 39:12).

Normally, I wouldn't have been brave enough to venture out onto the unlit country roads, but this prompting from the Spirit gave me courage beyond my own. I realized that I felt more concerned about what was inside my house than what I would find outside. I threw open my front door, sprinted down the driveway, and raced out onto the road.

As I ran, a hymn poured into my mind. It was as if a choir was singing to me: "The Lord is my light, then why should I fear, by day and by night, his presence is near."[7] Breathless from running, I could still hear the words of this hymn sounding over and over in my head. The music continued until I was ready to turn around and go home.

---

[7] "The Lord Is My Light," *Hymns*, no. 89.

I felt trepidation as I walked back into my house, but as soon as I pushed open the front door, I was no longer nervous. I knew I was safe.

I have often heard people quote the scripture in the New Testament that says, "But God is faithful, who will not suffer you to be tempted above that ye are able" (1 Corinthians 10:13). That scripture never made sense to me because I saw so many people around me succumb to sin. But studying the Book of Mormon clarified it for me, as it has clarified so many other scriptures. In order to receive the blessing of being protected against temptation, we have some work we need to do. For example, Alma explains "But that ye would humble yourselves before the Lord, and call on his holy name, and watch and pray continually, *that ye may not be tempted above that which ye can bear*" (Alma 13:28, italic added by author). Here, Alma identifies four things required to overcome temptation. Fortunately for me, I felt prompted to pray.

My prayer was heard and answered in a miraculous way that night. Again, I came to know for myself that not only does God hear and answer prayers, but that He truly knows each one of us, and our circumstances. If we will continue to call upon Him, He will bless, nurture, and watch over us.

After this incident in my home, living the Word of Wisdom became even more important to me. I learned that it is a commandment with a blessing and a promise. The blessing is that those who obey "Shall receive health in their navel and marrow to their bones; And shall find great treasures of knowledge, even hidden treasures, And shall run and not be weary, and shall walk and not faint."

The promise is "that the destroying angel shall pass by them, as the children of Israel, and not slay them" (D&C 89:18-21).

The day that I had this skirmish with an unseen force, I received hidden knowledge. I was able to see that even though the adversary was there enticing me, the Lord's Spirit would always be available to help, guide, and protect.

While I was in high school my friends and I were out together on a summer evening and later that night went to a friend's home who wasn't a member of the church. When someone pulled alcohol out of the refrigerator and started to pass it around, I decided to leave the house in order to adhere to my principles. This was before cell phones, and I had to walk down some dimly lit streets to get to a hotel and borrow a phone to call for a ride home. I was particularly frightened because a young woman had recently been murdered in our town while she was going to the grocery store at night.

Perhaps the earlier experience strengthened me to be able to go out on that unfamiliar street to avoid a spiritually dangerous situation. I believe that each confrontation that we overcome prepares us for future challenges. The Lord is always lighting our path in the present and for the future. I am grateful for the spiritual and temporal safety I had in both instances. The Lord most surely is our light and "walking by faith, I am blest ev'ry hour."

Fabulous Friends

One of my constant prayers through junior high and high school was to be given good friends. Later when I had graduated and gone to college, I wondered why I had prayed so hard on that subject. I had the best friends a person could desire. My close companions were all members of the church, and being around them, and especially their parents and their families, had a lasting impact on my thoughts and my decisions.

Perhaps I hadn't awarded enough credit to the Lord for hearing and answering this particular petition. He had given me the perfect people in my life. They helped protect me and nurture my testimony, and all the while I just thought that it was one of those random appeals that really didn't accomplish anything. Now I think differently. I know that I had such great friends because I asked for them, and because He knew they would be important for my future and my faith.

Friends not only guide our decisions about where we go and what we do, but they also provide mirrors for us. In the beginning of the twentieth century, a sociologist name Charles Horton Cooley developed the concept of the "Looking Glass Self." He postulates that our self-esteem is often formulated by the response of others. What he suggests is that everyone around us holds up a mirror for us to see ourselves. They do this by the responses they provide for our actions.

When we are selecting people to be our friends, we are essentially choosing mirrors. Do those that we bring into our lives to be our friends and our associates give us positive messages about ourselves, or do they drag us down with negative responses and attitudes? Examining the influence that people have on us as they provide mirrors can allow us to make better decisions about who we empower with our self-esteem and our lives.[8]

In addition to the concept of people as our mirrors, I learned in the book *Baby Steps to Happiness* more about how important it is to create intimate relationships carefully: "Choose your friends wisely. One of the most important decisions you will ever make is your choice of friends. The closer they are, the more important they become. The boundaries of friendship eventually become blurred. You influence your friends and they influence you."[9]

Julie Cameron in her book, *The Artist's Way*, encourages her readers to surround themselves with personalities who lift and encourage growth. Wouldn't it be great to find others who are interested in growing and improving themselves? One of my favorite quotes from Cameron's book comes from the Talmud: "Every blade of grass has its Angel that bends over it and whispers 'Grow, Grow.' "[10] We need to find friends, who help us to become

---

[8] Charles Horton Cooley, "Human Nature and the Social Order," *Scribner's Magazine* (New York: Charles Scribner's Sons, 1902): 179-185.

[9] John Q Baucom, *Baby Steps to Happiness* (Lancaster, Pennsylvania: Starburst Publishers, 1996), 167.

[10] Julie Cameron, *The Artist's Way* (New York City, New York: A Jeremy P. Tarcher/Putnam Book, 1992), 3.

better, the very best version of ourselves. We should surround ourselves with fabulous friends.

There are other influences we have in our lives, and it is important to make sure that these "friends" are a positive example. For instance, books, movies, television, and the internet can guide us toward good or evil. In the Book of Mormon Abinadi accuses King Noah and his perverse priests of surrounding themselves with wickedness. He says, "I perceive that ye have studied and taught iniquity the most part of your lives" (Mosiah 13:11). Learning, as we know, occurs in more than just a formal classroom setting. Sometimes our companions are those characters in the media with whom we choose to spend time. We learn from these scriptures that one of the ways people became evil is by "studying evil all their lives." When we sit down to a movie or when we read a book, are we studying evil? Are we watching or reading about how people live who are obeying a telestial law? Is there something fascinating about their lives that we want to study and emulate? Do these hours watching works of iniquity edify and enhance our lives, or do they cause us to dwindle in our beliefs, standards, and attitudes?

Unfortunately, we live in a day when it is more difficult than ever to find worthy examples in the material we read or watch. We must remember to choose all our chums cautiously no matter what form they take.

In the pamphlet, *For the Strength of Youth*, we read, "Everyone needs good and true friends. They will be a great strength and blessing to you. They will influence how you think and act, and even help determine the person you will become. They will help you be a better person and will make it easier for you to live the gospel of Jesus Christ.

Choose friends who share your values so you can strengthen and encourage each other in living high standards."[11] This is good advice for everyone, no matter what our age.

In the book of James, we learn about our most important friend. We read: "And the scripture was fulfilled which saith, Abraham believed God, and it was imputed unto him for righteousness; and he was called the Friend of God" (James 2:23). Of all those affiliations that we might want to cultivate around us, the best would be these: our Heavenly Father and His Son, Jesus Christ, and the Holy Ghost. The Savior teaches us, "Ye are my friends, if ye do whatsoever I command you" (John 15:14).

I am grateful that I was directed by the Spirit to continue to pray for good friends, and that those prayers were answered in amazing and miraculous ways. My friends, old and new, still affect me every day.

---

[11] *For the Strength of Youth* (Salt Lake City, Utah: The Church of Jesus Christ of Latter-day Saints, Intellectual Reserve, Inc. 2011), 16.

The Surprising Power of Satan

I attended Rick's College (now BYU-Idaho) for two years before graduating and going to Brigham Young University. I lived with wonderful roommates who were fun, encouraging, and spiritually strong in the gospel.

One night I had an experience that I will never forget because it taught me the surprising power of Satan. My roommate, Anita, and I shared a dorm room, and we had our beds against the wall meeting in the corner. Our heads were almost together with only a tiny table between us for lamps, clocks, and books.

Anita and I were both making preparations to go to bed, and we continued to talk as we lay down and pulled the covers over us. We often had nightly conversations discussing what had transpired during the day. I rolled over on my back and was preparing to go to sleep, but I knew Anita was still awake. Suddenly I felt a heavy weight on my chest. I tried to roll over to ask for her help, but I couldn't move. I was paralyzed. Then I thought I would call to her and explain that something was wrong.

When I tried to speak, I couldn't produce a peep. I was very frightened. It felt like there was only one thing to do, and that was to pray. I began to silently call on Heavenly Father for His help, and to ask Him for an escape from the situation that had taken control of both my body and my voice. After praying, I had a short loss of consciousness, and finally I was released. Then, I turned to tell Anita what had just happened to me.

Later, I shared with a friend on campus the details of this harrowing experience. I was informed that they had heard of other Rick's College students who also had this frightening event too. I have heard different theories about what is really happening when this occurs, but for me it was very clear that a power of evil had overcome me. Since I still had command of my thoughts, and because I was able to pray, I received the release that I desired.

My inspiration to pray came in part from remembering the experience of Joseph Smith in the grove of trees: "I was seized upon by some power which entirely overcame me, and had such an astonishing influence over me as to bind my tongue so that I could not speak" (JS-H-1:15).

Some people say that Satan, or the devil as he is also called, is not real. However we read in the Bible Dictionary: "Latter-day revelation confirms the biblical teaching that the devil is a reality and that he does strive to lead men and women from the work of God…Since the devil and his pre-mortal angels have no physical body of flesh and bones, they often seek to possess the bodies of mortal beings."[12]

Since we know that he does exist, we believe that he will use any tactic available against us. Thankfully, the gospel reveals to us the reality of Satan and also his techniques. If he cannot convince us that there is no such thing as a devil, then he may try to either frighten us, or to persuade us that he has ability to overcome us physically as he did in my case.

---

[12] See "Devil," Bible Dictionary, *The Holy Bible* (Salt Lake City, Utah: The Church of Jesus Christ of Latter-day Saints, 1979), 656.

This sober warning from President James E. Faust has real meaning to me. He said, "I think we will witness increasing evidence of Satan's power as the kingdom of God grows stronger. I believe Satan's ever-expanding efforts are some proof of the truthfulness of this work. In the future, the opposition will be both more subtle and more open. It will be masked in greater sophistication and cunning, but it will also be more blatant. We will need greater spirituality to perceive all of the forms of evil and greater strength to resist it."[13]

In my case, I came to believe early in my life that Satan is real, but I know that he does not have greater power than our Father in Heaven. Through prayer we always have access to our heavenly source of protection, and are able to be rescued from so many of the problems we encounter.

---

[13] James A. Faust, "Serving the Lord and Resisting the Devil," *Ensign*, September 1995.

But a Small Moment

After my first semester at Brigham Young University, and upon turning 21 years old, I decided to go on a mission. I was called to serve in the California North Mission. My second assigned area was in one of the Walnut Creek wards. I had just been transferred from Danville. While I was serving there in Walnut Creek, I was given an experience that is written on my soul.

I had come into the mission field so recently that I was still not sure how to do the work. My new companion didn't know the members in our ward at all, or what to do either. I began to feel pretty discouraged.

Then I started getting this incredible pain along my jaw whenever I ate anything hot or cold. It was so terrible that I was nearly incapacitated. I tried to be very careful about eating any foods that seemed to have very much temperature variation. I wrote to my mission president, Ira Terry, about my pain and I started praying to the Lord about my situation. I didn't think my companion and I were accomplishing very much, and now I could hardly do anything at all. The work was suffering from these problems.

My zone leader, knowing that I had been a cheerleader at Rick's College, told me that I wasn't having success because I was too proud. I was hurt by his comment because I didn't feel like I was a prideful person. He didn't know very much about me, or my life, so I didn't think he could properly ascertain the amount of pride I had, but it was still hard to hear. We were also living in sparse

circumstances in a little drab motel in the middle of Walnut
Creek, which felt pretty humble to me.

The combination of these five conditions: being new in
the mission field, having an inexperienced companion,
being accused of being prideful, living in substandard
housing, and now having such severe pain created a perfect
storm for me, and I knelt down and cast my burdens upon
the Lord. I told Him I wasn't happy, I wasn't doing any
good as a missionary, I didn't think I was qualified to do
the work, and that I was in a lot of pain. I don't remember
how long I prayed, but I got an answer.

The Spirit whispered that it "shall be but a small
moment" (D&C 121:7). I wasn't sure at the time what the
Lord meant, but I didn't stop to contemplate it right then. I
just wondered if I had I actually heard the voice of the Lord
before? I don't think so, because I was startled when I
received that real voice in my mind.

My mission president was a retired executive at General
Electric and had been involved in some way with the
development of the electric toothbrush. Because of his
background, he asked me to go see a dental practitioner in
the area. The dentist discovered that because I had a great
deal of work done on my teeth just before coming on my
mission, that my bite had not been adjusted properly and
that this was causing the pain. It was temporomandibular
joint dysfunction. As soon as it was diagnosed and
corrected, I was immediately better.

There were other challenges over the next 18 months in
the mission field, but as the years have come and gone, I
have found that my time in the California North Mission
was such miniscule section in the larger scope of my life:
"such a small moment."

The crowning jewel of that miraculous moment was actually hearing the voice of the Lord. It wasn't a thought. It was a clear voice in my mind. Is there a God? Yes, I have heard His voice. And what did He say? Scripture! He still speaks to me every time I open the standard works.

That divine voice is available to everyone as they read and study the scriptures. The Doctrine and Covenants bears this witness to us, "Wherefore the voice of the Lord is to the ends of the earth, that all that will hear may hear" (D&C 1:11). It has been said that if we want to speak to the Lord we pray, and if we want to hear His voice we read scripture. I know this is true. Whether that communication occurs in our minds or in our hearts, (D&C 8:2) it will always be a miraculous moment.

The One

While I was serving in Placerville, California my companion and I held a monthly meeting for those called as ward missionaries. We would either teach an inspirational message or work on methods for sharing the gospel in more effective ways. There were three or four members who had been called to serve in this way.

One night we went to the ward building to meet with the missionaries and only one sister came. We waited awhile and still no one else arrived. For some reason we decided that since only one person came we would not have a lesson, and we let her go home.

Since then, I have learned the influence that one person can have for good. That one woman may have learned something that would have helped her as a member or as a missionary. She may have had a faith-promoting story or scripture to share that would have either edified or energized us to be better missionaries.

I don't know what the results may have been if we had decided to teach just that one sister. But I have never underestimated the value of "the one" since then. I never make a decision on whether to go forward with an activity or a lesson based on the number of people present. Each person is precious to the Lord, and He values us on an individual basis and not just collectively.

The story of Alma demonstrates the power of teaching the one. When Alma heard the words of Abinadi, he knew that what was spoken was true. Making a personal declaration about this message almost cost Alma his life.

But his works, teachings, and visions permeate the Book of Mormon, and convince me that amazing miracles can be brought about by one person with a testimony (Mosiah 17:2-4). This is especially true if the one person who is taught goes forth to teach others, as this woman most surely would have done as a ward missionary.

The scriptures are filled with stories of "the one." Moses was just one man in Pharaoh's court, but he led the Israelites out of bondage. Abraham was just one man, but he became the father of nations. Many stories in the scriptures deal with just one person, and yet the impact that their life has on all of us is truly great; great to us, and great to the Lord.

The greatest One of all is the Savior, Jesus Christ. His one life and His one atonement have made the difference in both time and eternity. No "one" is more significant in what they have done for us than He is.

Throughout my life the example, and teachings of just one friend, just one teacher, just one speaker, or just one leader has been immeasurable in affecting my course. We should be aware that not only do other people do that for us, but we also can do the same for them.

The Lord clearly asks us to "remember the worth of souls is great in the sight of God" (D&C 18:10). I don't know what I would have taught or heard that night, but I know I learned the lesson of *The One* and I have always remembered it.

Our Picture with the Prophet

"Did you know President Kimball?" I am often asked when friends see our wonderful wedding picture.

"No," I answer, "I didn't know him." But then I have to explain that I was privileged to be involved in a circumstance which reminded me that not only was he a prophet but also a kind and caring man.

How often do ordinary members of the church have the opportunity to meet and shake hands with a prophet of God? How often does this kind of extraordinary event occur on one's wedding day? But this is exactly what happened to my husband and me.

Gary and I were married in the Salt Lake Temple on April 18, 1974. Our reception in the Jade Room of the Hotel Utah, now the Joseph Smith Building, followed later that day. It was a lovely evening and we were able to share it with our friends and family. We had no idea what was transpiring in other rooms nearby.

At about 9:00 p.m. as our event began to wind down, we noticed prominent brethren from the General Authorities pass by the open doors of our reception room. They seemed to be leaving a meeting that was held in a room next to ours. The last person to walk past our door was President Spencer W. Kimball.

Our best man spontaneously rushed over to see if President Kimball would take a picture with Gary and me. I was embarrassed. I would never have presumed to intrude on his time or to imposition him. President Kimball politely expressed that he had another meeting and that he was already a little late. He preceded forward a few steps, stopped, and then turned around and came back toward us to prepare to pose for the photographer.

Gary and I stood on both sides of President Kimball as our picture was taken. He then shook our hands as we explained to him that we had just been married in the Salt Lake Temple that day. All of this only took a few minutes, and then he was on his way.

I don't know what President Kimball was thinking when he turned back to take that picture. Did the Spirit give him an impression to return? Did he feel that this was a simple act of service that he could perform easily? I'm not sure. I'll never know what his motivation was for that choice.

However, when Gary and I had a moment to think about the time that we had with President Kimball and discuss it, we realized that the prophet, who was then in his 80th year, still had one more meeting that night even though it was already quite late in the evening. He truly was wearing out his life in service to the Lord. His motto to "Lengthen Your Stride" was one he personally lived.

How well this statement describes him: "Known for his humility, his commitment, his ability to work, and his personal slogan, 'Do It,' President Kimball thrust in his sickle with all his might."[14]

We loved to hear President Kimball speak, and we tried to do what he asked of us—first, because he was a prophet, and also because of the example he set in those brief

---

[14] *Doctrine and Covenants and Church History Student Study Guide* (Salt Lake City, Utah: The Church of Jesus Christ of Latter-day Saints, 2005), 207.

minutes we had together. I know that even small acts of kindness are important, are often remembered, and can impact our lives. Truly, "out of small things proceeded that which is great" (D&C 64:33).

Our wedding day became an even more amazing and eventful time for us because it was the day we had our picture taken with the prophet.

Not Today

During our first Christmas together, my husband, Gary, and I did what many BYU students do: we piled into the car with siblings and drove home.[15] For my husband, home is Minnesota, and it is a long and sometimes treacherous drive in the winter. It turned out that Christmas, cars, and four tired college kids created a perfect combination for a crisis.

We had been traveling for hours when Gary's sister, Connie, took over the driving at about 2 a.m. None of us remembered to check to see how much gas we had, but when she did finally notice, the gauge registered empty. She woke up all of us and we tried to decide what to do. We didn't think we had enough gas to make it to a service station in the next large town, so we exited the freeway. Unfortunately, all the stations nearby were closed.

The only thing to do was to keep driving. The country lane we drove down to the next town was very dark and deserted. The temperature in Nebraska that night was frigid: double digits below zero. And then, we ran out of gas and the car stopped.

What would we do now? We decided that Gary and his brother, Lee, would have to find some gas. They got out of the car and walked toward the closest lights they saw down the road in the distance. Connie and I stayed in the car and

---

[15] See original publication: Gail H. Johnsen, "Don't Overlook Opportunities to Serve," *Deseret News*, December 11, 2011.

prayed. I was six months pregnant with our first child. I was cold and scared.

Gary and Lee came to a farmhouse about a mile away from our car. They woke up the resident of the house and told him our situation. They asked him to sell them just enough gas to get to a station. His response was surprising: "Not today."

"Not today?" the brothers thought as they walked back to the car. After telling Connie and I their story, they went to the next closest farm that was about a mile in the other direction where they were able to buy both gas and a gas can from a kind and sympathetic farmer. Then they trudged to the car again. They were able to get enough fuel so we could make it to an open gas station. More than forty years have passed since we asked that first farmer for gas. We have never been back to ask him if "today" might be the right day.

At the time, we were disappointed and couldn't believe that this man wasn't willing to help us. Over the years though, I have realized that often we are like that farmer— waiting for convenient moments to serve. My husband and I have found that there will always be opportunities in our lives to help others, but certain moments in time, and various kinds of possibilities, only come along once in a lifetime.

We have also learned that service often requires sacrifice, and I truly believe that this is the best kind of service because it brings with it the blessings of heaven.[16]

Elder Dallin H. Oaks reminds us, "Our Savior teaches us to follow him by making the sacrifices necessary to lose

---

[16] "Praise to the Man," *Hymns, no. 27.*

ourselves in unselfish service to others. If we do, he promises us eternal life, 'Which gift is the greatest of all the gifts of God' " (D&C 14:7).[17]

---

[17] Dallin H. Oaks, "Unselfish Service," E*nsign,* May 2009.

His Healed Hand

Wyoming winters are very cold, and the wind howls thunderously around houses and farms. Our young family, which at that time consisted of four young boys, spent most of our time in the house when the temperatures dropped down below zero in Gillette. To warm ourselves, our living room featured a prominent wood burning stove. We had central heating but used the stove too.

One winter, when our tiny toddler, Clay, was still crawling but learning how to pull himself up on the furniture in order to come to a standing position, I was reminded what a blessing it is to have the priesthood in my home.

On a Sunday afternoon everyone, including my husband who was in the Bishopric, was home. I didn't feel very well and had decided to go up to my bedroom to rest. I was always worried about the stove and how dangerous it was. The older children all knew that they were to stay completely away from it in the winter. It was a glowing, scorching red hot when it was full of wood and a fire was blazing.

I had put everyone on alert to tend Clay but I wasn't specific enough about who was actually the person assigned to watch him. I hadn't been in my bed very long before I heard a deafening scream come from the living room. I knew immediately from the earsplitting sound and from the location exactly what had happened. I was off that bed like a shot exploding from a firearm. It is amazing how quickly a person can move even when they don't feel well.

I was down those eight steps and gathering the baby into my arms almost immediately. I don't know where my husband had been, but he appeared shortly afterwards as well.

Clay had crawled across the room and put his hand directly on the stove to pull himself up. After the first shriek and his recognition of pain, he sobbed uncontrollably. I immediately inspected his little hand and large blisters had begun to appear. My husband dashed to our bedroom to get his consecrated oil.

I placed Clay on my lap and my husband put both hands on his small head and began to administer to him. Almost immediately his crying stopped, and then a sweet stillness encircled us. It was as if there was no pain at all. After the blessing, we rushed to a friend's house nearby who was a nurse. She examined his hand and gave us ointment and gauze to clean and dress the wound. We did this for several days.

Clay only had minor scarring from his burn, which is amazing to me; but the miracle that day was that a little 10-month-old baby, who knew nothing about the priesthood blessing that was being administered to him, would stop wailing as hands were laid upon his head.

We learn from the scriptures that, "All blessings are based on eternal laws (D&C 130:20–21). Because God wants his children to find joy in life (2 Ne. 2:25), he grants blessings to them as a result of their obedience to his commandments (D&C 82:10), in answer to a prayer or priesthood ordinance (D&C 19:38; 107:65–67)."[18]

---

[18] See "Bless, Blessed, Blessing," *The Guide to the Scriptures* (Salt Lake City, Utah: The Church of Jesus Christ of Latter-day Saints).

What a miracle to have such power available to us right in our own homes. Within seconds we can call down the blessings of heaven upon our family. We felt very thankful that day for all the gospel brings into our lives.

The Gift of the Milk Pitcher

One freezing and frosty Christmas when our family lived in Gillette, Wyoming, I received a present that truly was a heavenly gift.[19] As a young mother of four small boys, my days were filled with what seemed like a daunting work load. Then, the holiday season added more cooking, shopping, and lots of decorating. I hadn't taken the time to think about, or request, any special Christmas gifts for myself. My husband was very busy at work and had been asked to put in some overtime. He also had a great deal of church work, which made it difficult to think about gift giving or to spend time shopping.

Despite our lack of planning, Christmas did finally arrive and with it the opening of presents. I found that my husband had given me two gifts: one was a new waffle iron and the other a very ugly, mustard-colored pitcher for mixing milk. We combined our powered milk with whole milk that was purchased at the grocery store as a strategy for rotating our food storage and for saving money. I don't think the pitcher cost over $2.

After opening these offerings, I was hurt. I suddenly realized that I didn't want a waffle iron for a gift. It was a work tool. I wanted something for myself, a gift that said I was a person, not just a cook. The real problem though was the budget pitcher. I don't know what my husband was thinking when he bought it, but if he had known how I

[19] See original publication: Gail H. Johnsen, "The Gift of the Milk Pitcher," *Deseret News*, December 26, 2009.

would react to that single selection, I am sure he would not have considered getting or giving it.

It was the first time I realized that the ideal gift was one that said, "I have taken some time thinking about you and what you would love, and I might have spent a few extra dollars on it because you are a treasure to me." This just hadn't been the year for it though.

The result of that particular present was that I couldn't speak to my husband for at least two weeks. I couldn't get over it. It was winter at our home, inside and out. Day after day I continued to feel hurt—hurt to the core. But I began to see that we couldn't possibly go on like this forever, and I wanted to forgive him, but I simply couldn't figure out how to do it.

One day, while wishing I could change things, I suddenly decided I needed to pray about this problem. When the thought occurred to me, I dropped to my knees right where I was standing in my living room and leaned against my couch. I told my Heavenly Father that I was too injured, I couldn't forgive my husband, or that I didn't know how to forgive him, and would He please help me.

Suddenly I felt warmth pouring into my heart, and I knew that real healing was taking place. I was no longer suffering, experiencing disappointment, or feeling upset with my husband. These emotions had been taken away completely. I recognized that not only a spiritual, but also a physical change had occurred within me. This was a far greater gift than any I might have anticipated that year. It included the reminder that God does hear and answer prayers, that He can heal His children, and that He takes an active interest in our lives and in our marriages.

Since that time I have prayed about many kinds of healings and found that the Lord does not always cure all our wounds immediately, and that I have to learn patience and trust in Him. This too has increased and strengthened my faith. But I will always remember that one Christmas Heavenly Father saw my disappointment and gave me not only the gift of His Son, Jesus Christ, but also an unexpected gift of healing.

Finding My Father

A Primary song that is often sung in the church is, "I Am a Child of God." It supports the idea that we are children of a personal Heavenly Father. We sing these words:

I am a child of God,
And he has sent me here,
Has given me an earthly home
With parents kind and dear.
Lead me, guide me, walk beside me
Help me find the way.
Teach me all that I must do
To live with him someday.[20]

This favorite children's tune also suggests that we have earthly parents who are kind and dear. What a wonderful thought! However, sometimes the ideal clashes with reality and then we have to decide how to handle the difference.

One of those decisions occurred after I had started dating a young man who I met in my first area while in the mission field. I saw him several times after that; once while he was an Assistant to the President. He was a very enthusiastic and hardworking missionary. When we started dating at BYU, he was working on a Masters of Accountancy degree. After we got engaged I felt that I was

---

[20] "I am a child of God, " *Hymns,* no. 301.

going to marry a terrific person and went to tell my dad about him.

My father was not religious and was divorced from my mother. He wasn't the kind of person to whom I turned for help or advice, but I did want to share with him the good news of my engagement. His response was discouraging and rather denigrating to Gary, but just about what I had come to expect.

As the years went by, the things that my father had said about my future spouse had very little significance in my life; that is until I was praying one evening while I was living in Wyoming. For some reason that night I remembered a story that one of my BYU friends had told me about how President Hinckley had interviewed the prospective groom of one of his daughters. He wanted to make sure that the young man was a good candidate to marry her. Not only was that story on my mind, but I began to recall many of the other men that I knew that were excellent and exemplary fathers.

During this particular session of prayer, I began to feel sad and disappointed about the parent I had been given. It seemed so unfair. I wondered why I had him, and why others had an apostle for a father. I was kneeling down next to my bed talking to the Lord and feeling very dismayed. I began to ask the Lord why some people have such wonderful parents, while others had to suffer with those who don't provide helpful patterns to follow.

The intensity of my feelings drew me closer to the floor, and soon I was on my knees crying and praying with my face in my hands. Then in my anguish and confusion, I just laid flat on the floor with my face down. I was pleading with the Lord to help me understand this discrepancy. Then

I heard a clear voice in my mind that would change my life and my perspective forever. "I am your Father; Man of Holiness is my name." This was a very distinct and miraculous moment for me in understanding who I am, and who my true Father really is.

Our circumstances in life may sometimes seem unfair, and I know that not every child sent into the world will have parents that are kind and dear, whether they are members of the church or not. I know that as more homes become dysfunctional, less and less children will find a family that provides proper care and nurturing. How important it is to share this gospel with others so they can understand their true relationship with Heavenly Father.

I also know that it was not the manner in which I prayed or the position of my body that made the difference that night, but I believe I must have been praying in accordance with His will. In 1 John it says, "And this is the confidence that we have in him, that, if we ask any thing according to his will, he heareth us" (1 John 5:14).

We also can be taught by the Spirit how to pray, and are given the very words to utter. Modern-day scriptures instruct us that "it shall be given you what you shall ask;" (D&C 50:30). As I liken these words of revelation given through the Prophet Joseph Smith to myself, I feel that the Spirit can at times teach me what to say in my prayers.

That day as I prayed, I understood that I had a parent that was the Parent of all Parents. I was truly a child of God, and even though many of us will be sent to earth with situations that are not perfect, our true parent will always be our Father in Heaven. Truly, I am a child of God.

An Increase

I am sure that I knelt many times in prayer while I was living in Wyoming, and I don't recall very much of the content of these hours of expressed gratitude or earnest supplication. But there were a few that I remember distinctly. I could not possibly forget them.

Unfortunately, I don't know the exact subject of my thoughts as I knelt down to pray one day. I know I was on the second floor of the house and in my bedroom. At this point in my life, I seldom had a time that I didn't have preschoolers or babies at home. In my memory, I was able to pray that day uninterrupted by anyone. Perhaps it was during my children's nap time, or it might have been in the evening. I only remember that I had a rare private moment for a mother, and I was alone.

While I was in a quiet attitude of pondering, I discovered something happening to the top of my head. The best way I can describe it would be to picture opening the lid on a can of food. Most of the time, we open a can only about 90% of the way and then lift the lid. This is how it felt to me. It seemed like the crown of my head was being opened and peeled back. I was very mystified by this feeling, and then even more perplexed by what followed. I perceived that light was pouring into my brain through a pillar that came down from heaven. It was as if a funnel of luminance was filtering down into my mind like a stream of water from a pitcher. Then just as suddenly, the light was gone, and the lid that had been opened was closed.

Later I read that there is a surgery called craniotomy. It is an operation in which a bone flap is temporarily removed from the skull to access the brain. Typically the bone flap is replaced. I suppose that what I experienced might be considered a spiritual craniotomy. Also, today lasers are commonly used as a form of light amplification for many amazing purposes, including healing. At that time, the only pillar of light that I knew about was the one from Joseph Smith's first vision (JS-H 1:16).

I don't really know what changed for me after this happened, but it was as if whatever had been left out, or whatever was needed for my life, was put in and was added to my mind and perhaps my body. I didn't notice any radical changes in my behavior, talents, or dedication to my family or to the gospel at that time. But over the years, I have felt that my talents and abilities have gone far beyond what I actually anticipated when I was younger. I feel I have been able to endure things that I never could have handled without extra help. I have always assumed that the Lord gave me an "increase" that day.

The scriptures teach this: "I have planted, Apollos watered; but God gave the increase" (1 Cor. 3:6). If I plant, which to me means to work, to study, and to be steadfast in my convictions, the Lord can give an increase—in any way that He desires. The scripture that follows says, "So then neither is he that planteth any thing, neither he that watereth; but God that giveth the increase" (1 Cor. 3:7). This is a great reminder about the source of all gifts and blessings.

Although the Lord provides the increase, I also need to participate to make my life the best it can be. One of my favorite ideas about how we can set goals and enhance our individual capacity comes from the book, *I Dare You!* by William H. Danforth.[21] He created the Ralston's checkerboard logo which he felt encapsulated all the important principles in life. If one can picture a square and inside that square are four smaller squares, you have the checkerboard square concept. Each individual square represents a key area in our lives; from left to right proceeding around the square they represent physical, mental, social, and religious. To truly flourish, we need to set goals in all four squares. One area is not to develop at the expense of the other. This concept became intertwined with the company in 1921 when it began selling animal feed that was pressed into cubes called checkers. I think the reason I like it so much is because in the scriptures we are told that the Savior also had increases in his life, "And Jesus increased in wisdom and stature, and in favor with God and man" (Luke 2:52). Interestingly, these four areas correspond to Danforth's categories—Wisdom (mental), stature (physical), in favor with God (religious), and man (social). Unfortunately the term which Danforth used of being square now has negative connotations. Today we say that someone is well-rounded or has a very balanced life.

As we seek to set goals and to increase our capabilities, these four areas could be the basis for improvement in our lives. I have set my goals using this precept for many years because I believe it was the standard that the Savior subscribed to in his own life.

Along with my own efforts to improve myself, the Lord also saw fit to give me an increase. Perhaps I would have been able to accomplish all I needed to do without this

---

[21] William H. Danforth, *I Dare You!* (New York City, New York: Cosimo Classic, 2007; originally published in 1953).

help, but I can state unequivocally that something went in that wasn't there before. I felt it.

The Errand of Angels

Many of our Family Home Evenings were memorable to me as a mother, but one particular Monday night stands out.[22] I had prepared a lesson from the Book of Mormon about Nephi and his brothers. I wanted to emphasize the principle of obedience in such a way that my children would remember how important it is to keep the Lord's commandments. I hoped that they would also recognize the blessings associated with this gospel precept. That evening, however, I was the one who learned a valuable lesson.

My husband and I gathered our four young boys together in the family room. I sat on the couch and my boys sat cross-legged on the floor in front of me. I explained that Nephi demonstrated his obedience to both his father and to the Lord when he agreed to return to Jerusalem to obtain the brass plates. Despite the difficulty and the distance, Nephi declares, "I will go and do the things which the Lord hath commanded" (1 Nephi 3:7). With only a minimum of tussling, my children sat quietly as I told them this story.

Next, I explained that after several attempts to accomplish their purpose, the brothers had to flee Laban's house without the gold and silver that they brought from their home. They had neither the plates nor their worldly wealth, and they were angry. Blaming their father and their brother, the scriptures say that Laman and Lemuel were speaking harshly to Nephi and Sam, and then they began to smite them with a rod.

---

[22] See original publication: Gail H. Johnsen, "The Errand of Angels" *Deseret News*, July 10, 2011.

Now I had my family's full attention! What happened when the older boys were hitting their younger brothers? "An angel of the Lord came and stood before them, and he spake unto them saying: Why do ye smite your younger brother with a rod?" (1 Nephi 3:29). At that moment the similarities between those four sons of Lehi, and my four sons, became a little more apparent. I turned to my husband who was sitting next to me and quietly said, "Sometimes I wish an angel would come down here and stop the fighting."

Before my husband could respond, my eight-year-old son, Clark, said to me, "Mom, you're the angel."

"Me, an angel?" I wondered. I didn't feel like one. But then I asked myself, "What work do angels perform?" Among other responsibilities, angels are messengers from the Lord, and they minister to His children. Surely, these definitions bear a close resemblance to the lives of righteous women and their good works. Women have opportunities to teach, nurture, and care for Heavenly Father's children. I felt touched and inspired by my son's comment.

Now, whenever I sing the second verse of "As Sisters in Zion" these words emphasize for me the significance of my experience: "The errand of angels is given to women; And this is a gift that as sisters, we claim: To do whatsoever is gentle and human, To cheer and to bless in humanity's name."[23]

President James E. Faust cemented this concept for me when he said, "May you have an eternal perspective as you go about your angelic cause of doing good so that it will

---

[23] "As Sisters in Zion," *Hymns*, no. 309.

not only lead you to become great women but ultimately to become queens in the eternities."[24]

This was a small but miraculous moment in my life. I was reminded of the importance of my role as a mother and also my opportunities as a woman in Zion. I know that it is a privilege to be able to bless my Heavenly Father's children throughout my life.

---

[24] James A. Faust, "How Near to the Angels," *New Era,* March 1999.

They Were Listening

It was stake conference for the Fair View Heights
Illinois Stake.[25] To attend, our family had to travel an hour
and a half to get to St. Louis where the stake center was
located. At that time my husband and I had five children,
who ranged in age from about 12 months to 12 years old.
The children were usually ready to run and play by the time
we arrived, but we still had the entire meeting ahead of us.

This particular Sunday, I had to manage the entire group
by myself because my husband, Gary, was singing in the
stake choir. I was prepared with scripture-based coloring
books and quiet toys because I knew my children would
struggle to be reverent through the two-hour service. I was
a little anxious about my ability to handle this task.

I found seats for my family in the overflow section of
the chapel so that we might not be disruptive to others, and
hoped that I would be able to glean something from the
messages while I attended to my children's needs. I placed
the three older children to the right of me and the two
youngest on my left side.

The stake presidency had assigned a young married
sister to address us. She had been asked to speak about how
to cultivate and maintain love in our marriages. I had just
looked down to check my children and although they were
quiet, they didn't seem to be paying attention to the speaker
at all. As a matter of fact, from their faces and their
occupations at the time, I felt quite certain that they were

[25] See original publication: Gail H. Johnsen, "The Right Place at the
Right Time," *Deseret News,* September 5, 2009.

not listening to one word she was saying. Then the sister said that good marriages included, "warm, affectionate sex."

I was looking and listening to the speaker, but with my peripheral vision, I saw several heads jerk in my direction. I turned to see what had caused the reaction and saw wide eyes staring at me. My oldest son leaned closer and whispered, "She said sex!"

Since that day, I have felt sure that children hear a lot more in church than we think they do. I have felt that it will always be important to be in the right place at the right time. As Sister Elaine L. Jack expressed in her talk entitled, "Walk with Me": "We've been given tools to develop that spirituality. We are told to attend church meetings, work hard in callings, go to the temple, be generous in offering to the Lord, hold family home evening and visit one another. But simply being there does not sanctify us; statistics do not drive eternal progression. Still, we cannot ignore that being in the right place at the right time will put us in a frame of mind to learn, in an environment where the Lord's influence is invited and strong."[26]

Coming to church can develop into all kinds of learning experiences, and even though some of our activities there are not ideal because we may spend some of our time in the mother's lounge, walking the halls with a fussy baby, or wrestling tired children through Sacrament meeting, I believe that we may all learn and feel more than we think. I also hope to set an example of consistent attendance in church that may influence my family and give them a solid

---

[26] Elaine L. Jack, "Walk with Me," *Ensign,* May 1994.

foundation of gospel activity. I continually pray that I will be found doing the right thing, in the right place, and the right time.

Whited Sepulchers

In the Midwest, spring storms sweep through small communities often leaving destruction in their wake.[27] Our family felt the full force of such an event while we were living in Illinois. One morning the town's emergency siren sounded, alerting citizens of the severe weather conditions. I rushed Zane and Karen, my two youngest children, to the lowest level of my home to seek shelter as torrential rain, hail, and damaging winds blasted over businesses and residences alike. When the storm subsided, we ventured upstairs and outside to survey the scene. Trees littered the ground, and leaves, stripped from branches, were plastered to the siding of our home. Many of the screens on our windows were ripped open and we found hail on the inside of window ledges.

Shortly thereafter, panicky parents converged on schools to pick up their children. Frantic mothers descended *en masse* and found their students huddled in hallways because classrooms were full of shattered glass from broken windows. I was among this anxious group.

After all my children were safely stowed in our car, instead of going straight home, we decided to discover what damage had been done and began to drive around town. Although debris littered lawns and roads everywhere, the streets were mostly passable.

As we neared the courthouse, we saw that a stately tree lay like a fallen friend in the middle of the lawn. It had a

---

[27] See original publication: Gail H. Johnsen. "A Fallen Tree and a Whited Sepulcher," *Deseret News*, April 11, 2011.

massive trunk and must have stood there for many years providing summer shade and beauty to the area. We knew the winds alone could not have produced these results, so we clamored out of our car to get a closer look.

What we found startled all of us. The inside of the tree was completely hollow. What had occurred? Perhaps termites had gradually gobbled up the interior over the years. Or was it some kind of beetle or an undetected tree disease? We didn't know.

While the tree looked impressive on the outside, it could not withstand the powerful storm. It reminded me of a moment in the Savior's life when he denounced those who appear to be one thing, but were really something else. He said, "Woe unto you, Scribes and Pharisees and hypocrites! for ye are like unto whited sepulchers, which indeed appear beautiful outward, but are within full of dead man's bones and of all uncleanness" (Matt 23:27).

In his talk, "The Practice of Truth," Bishop J. Richard Clark reminds us, "Our souls must be more than 'whited sepulchers' which appear praiseworthy but inside are hollow chambers bereft of goodness. We must not only seem but also be what God would expect of His sons and daughters."[28]

When the twin tempests of trial and temptation twirl around us, we can be assured that we will stand "steadfast and immovable, always abounding in good works"[29] as we keep clean the inner vessel by obeying the commandments and following the brethren.

---

[28] Richard J. Clarke, "The Practice of Truth," *Ensign,* May 1984.

[29] Mosiah 5:15

A Feeling of Family

On a beautiful June morning, all seven of my children and I began the first leg of a two-part journey.[30] It was the start of their summer vacation, and we were traveling to Utah where we planned to pick up the rest of our family. Then we were to continue on to Newport Beach, California for some relaxation and fun.

Late in the afternoon of that day we ran into some rain, which soon turned into hail. I had just been through a spring storm in Carlinville, Illinois where we lived, and it made me more aware of the damage hail could do. I quickly started looking for a place to park so that I could protect my family and my van. Fortunately there was a small slice of space left under an overpass nearby; several other cars had already parked there. Soon after stopping, I heard a loud siren. I unrolled my window and calling out over the boisterous wind, I asked the driver in the next car what the siren meant. He yelled back that it was a tornado warning from a town nearby.

I immediately instructed all the children to get under the blankets that were in the car; but before everyone was safely covered, the side windows were shattered by flying debris. My youngest child, Karen, who was about 18 months old at the time, was seated next to a window, so I frantically told my son, Clark, to pull both of them under a blanket. Before he was able to get completely covered though, he felt the effects of the flying glass and received

---

[30] See original publication: Gail H. Johnsen, "A Feeling of Family," *The Church News,* 1990.

some minor cuts. Two of the other children, Jocelyn and Zane, were under a blanket near the front, and I dived under it too.

I truly thought that we were all going to die. It was a very eerie sensation thinking that it may be my last few minutes on earth. Then I was told through the Spirit to do something that I had learned while I was attending the temple one day, and I believe it changed the course of the events and saved our lives. From that moment on I knew we would be safe. Unfortunately others nearby didn't fare as well. A semi-truck had flipped over on its side nearby, and damaged cars littered both lanes of the freeway. After the tornado passed by, some help arrived. A thoughtful truck driver stopped and gave us a warm blue blanket that he kept for possible emergencies. A policeman checked on us and asked if we were all okay.

Most of the windows in our van were broken, but thankfully not the front windshield, so we were legally allowed to drive. We found a hotel a few miles away but learned that there were no rooms available. We also discovered that the power, lights, and bathrooms weren't working either. However, the management allowed us and many other people to sleep in the lobby. It was a long night because we didn't have a flashlight, and so we couldn't see anything at all. I don't know if the boys slept, but Karen was not comfortable, and she fussed and squirmed and I didn't get any sleep at all that night.

When we were ready to leave the next morning, we found that someone had wrapped the windows of our vehicle with Saran Wrap to keep the rain out. With plastic wrap flying from the sides of the car, and the children looking quite forlorn all draped from head to toe with blankets to keep warm, we drove into Denver.

I found a business where I could make a phone call, and I discovered that the woman who worked there was a member of the church. When I told her about our situation, she called her Relief Society President. Together they found a body shop that would vacuum out the glass and replace all the windows on my van. Then the Relief Society President took us to her home.

This generous and caring woman helped us get cleaned up and we stayed at her house for several hours while the work was being done to our van. She fed our family and provided comfortable beds so that we were able to rest that afternoon. Even though we were complete strangers to this sister we were treated like family. As brothers and sisters in the gospel and as children of our Heavenly Father, our actions can create a strong feeling of family for members of The Church of Jesus Christ of Latter-day Saints. It is a unique and incredible advantage to be part of this amazing congregation of followers of the Savior.

Desirable and Delicious

Sunday is our family day, and it is wonderful just
spending time together. Since our ward always met in the
morning, we often had a big meal right after church, and
then snacks and family popcorn in the evening. As soon as
we arrived home one Sabbath my husband, Gary, began to
prepare food for the family, and I was setting the table for
the meal. Although I had done this many times before, this
Sunday I had an exquisite experience. In retrospect I
wonder what I was thinking about that day. What messages
had I heard at church that might have caused me to ponder
or prepare for this moment?

Suddenly I was filled with a sensation of complete love
that surged throughout my entire body. It was as if I were
being flooded with so much joy that I might explode. I have
never known anything like that before. I remembered that I
had read something similar in the Book of Mormon though.
Nephi explained what happened to him by saying "He hath
filled me with love, even unto the consuming of my flesh"
(2 Nephi 4:21).

Many people who have had a near-death event and are
met by a Being of Light try to explain the feeling of
complete, unconditional love that surrounds them. This is
how it felt to me—pure love pouring into my body and
spirit.

Since that time, I have a better understanding of the
story in the Book of Mormon about Lehi's dream of the
tree of life, and also the interpretation of it. Nephi states
"And the angel said unto me…Knowest thou the meaning

of the tree which thy father saw? And I answered him saying: Yea, it is the love of God, which sheddeth itself abroad in the hearts of men; wherefore, it is the most desirable above all things…Yea, and the most joyous to the soul" (1 Nephi 11:21-23). I can testify that the fruit of the tree is most desirable above all things. Knowing, really knowing, in a tangible way that the Lord loves me, is very desirable and delicious to my soul.

Alma explains his experience with the fruit of the tree when he says, "Now, when I think of the success of these my brethren my soul is carried away, even to the separation of my body, as it were, so great is my joy" (Alma 29:16).

What do the scriptures tell us we need to do to taste of the fruit? Just what dedicated members of the church do as a matter of course: we press forward and hold onto the iron rod. We keep the covenants we have made and obey the Lord's commandments. Partaking of the fruit of that tree, and knowing how much the Lord loves us, can certainly occur at some time for each of us because this dream of Lehi's shows us the course we should follow to be able to feel that love.

Why are these stories included in scripture? I don't think it is just because it is nice to know that other people have felt the love of the Lord in their own lives. Perhaps it is to show us that this manifestation is possible, and then to explain exactly how to make it happen. While the Lord wants all of us to feel His love, He cannot force it on us. He cannot make this a priority in our lives.

I see now why anyone who has felt this love and joy wants everyone to experience it. As Sister Bonnie D. Parkin, past Relief Society general president, explained: "If I could have one thing happen for every woman in this

Church, it would be that they would feel the love of the Lord in their lives daily. I have felt the love of the Lord in my life, and I am so thankful for that."[31] Like Sister Parkin, Lehi also had this strong desire. He says, "And as I partook of the fruit thereof it filled my soul with exceedingly great joy; wherefore, I began to be desirous that my family should partake of it also; for I knew that it was desirable above all other fruit" (1 Nephi 8:12).

Knowing that we are children of a Heavenly Father, tasting of the fruit, and feeling His love, can create a strong desire within us to share the gospel. We are going out in record numbers: young women, young men, older members and couples to tell the world of His love for all His children.

I didn't know then how very soon I would need to understand the power of the Lord's love for me, but the Lord knew. The scriptures testify "For he knoweth all things, and there is not anything save he knows it" (2 Nephi 9:20). That Sunday Heavenly Father allowed me to feel of His infinite love. I believe that the Lord does prepare us in advance for any problems or situations that we may encounter. As parents we can sometimes see what the future holds for our children, and we are constantly engaged in efforts to prepare and fortify them for upcoming challenges.

I can testify that partaking of this fruit is worth whatever we have to sacrifice or endure. Truly, it is as Nephi said, very desirable and delicious.

---

[31] Bonnie D. Parkin, "Feel the Love of the Lord," *Ensign*, May 2002.

Who Loves You?

During the seven years that we lived in Illinois we had many happy, and a few trying times. We were very busy because Gary served as Bishop, and I was the Primary President. We felt blessed to be able to assist in the work of the Lord. But my main responsibility was as a mother and occasionally I felt unequal to the task, and I struggled to raise our children correctly. I wondered if I was doing it the way that it should be done. After Gary was released from being the Bishop, he was called into the Stake High Council, which meant he would be away from home three of the four Sundays every month. Our stake had very large boundaries, and sometimes he had to travel over an hour each way to attend meetings in other buildings. We didn't get the extra time together that we anticipated when he was released as Bishop.

Because I was the one doing the majority of the parenting, these feelings of incompetence increased as it became evident that our children had some personal problems that we hadn't been able to diagnose. I just wasn't sure how to rear them properly, but I kept trying to learn and study. I spent a great deal of time reading books on parenting, and also on my knees petitioning the Lord for His help.

Sometime after having the blessing of being filled with Heavenly Father's love, I had what I would describe as a blatant attack by the adversary. The first experience prepared me for the second. I am sure Heavenly Father knew I would have this test, and had provided me with the necessary tools to combat the lies of Satan. As I said, it was a challenge raising my children, and I wasn't always sure that as a mother I was making the right decisions, and I sometimes felt overwhelmed.

One evening after the children were in bed and Gary was away from home, I went into my bathroom feeling very desolate and bereft. I was standing at first, and then lowered myself into a sitting position on the floor with my back against the wall, and I began to cry. It was one of those moments when I really wanted to wail, but with children in the next room I had to cry more quietly, which made my feelings more intense. I began to enumerate all the things that were wrong with me, and how poorly I was doing as a parent. The more I numbered these negative qualities, the worse I felt. Then even more ideas of faults and failings came flooding into my mind. Soon I was crouched on the floor in the fetal position feeling very distraught.

As I ticked off my defects one at a time, I said out loud to myself what I considered to be the fatal flaw, "And nobody even loves me." Suddenly, I shot up into a straight sitting position and looked around. I had just recently had the very powerful experience in which I KNEW that Heavenly Father loved me. I had felt it in every fiber of my being, and I could not deny it. At that moment, I realized that someone had just lied to me. Only Satan would have me feel that, miserable, and alone. I said a prayer and cast him out.

Since then I have found that when I am thinking positively about myself, I am in the presence of the Holy Ghost. A feeling of happiness and peace surrounds me. When I am feeling badly about myself, I believe I am in the presence of the adversary, and I say a prayer that I might be protected from his falsehood and deceptions.

I can personally attest to this statement by Richard C. Edgley: "Satan is the great deceiver, liar, and enemy to all that is good, including our happiness and our well-being. His great desire is to thwart our Heavenly Father's plan of happiness and make us 'miserable like unto himself' " (2 Ne. 2:27).[32]

President Ezra Taft Benson also warned us that this would be the case in the latter days: "Satan is increasingly striving to overcome the Saints with despair, discouragement, despondency, and depression."[33]

These additional thoughts by Jennifer Nuckols in her article "Truth and Lies" helped me understand even more methods used by Satan to undermine us:

"**The Lie**: Because of my weaknesses and failings, God is continually disappointed in, frustrated with, and even angry with me. **The Truth**: God loves me and rejoices in me because I am His child."

"**The Lie**: I'm not as righteous, spiritual, attractive, or kind as that other person; therefore, God must love that person more than He loves me. **The Truth**: God knows my individual potential and progress intimately. He does not compare or rank me with His other children."

"**The Lie**: I need to prove that I'm worth loving by being perfect. Only when I'm perfect will I be able to experience love from God and from others. **TheTruth:** Even though I'm not perfect now, I can have constant access to divine love."

---

[32] Richard C. Edgley, "Satan's Bag of Snipes," *Ensign,* November 2000.
[33] Ezra Taft Benson, "Do Not Despair," *Ensign*, November, 1974.

"**The Lie**: I'm a terrible failure. I'll never be good enough because I keep making the same mistakes over and over again. **The Truth**: I'm not perfect, but the desires of my heart are good. I can feel inspired to progress."

"**The Lie**: I have too many issues, hang-ups, and past mistakes to be blessed and happy. **The Truth**: No mistake, no personal challenge, no past circumstance is outside of the healing and redemptive power of the Atonement."[34]

I am sure that this isn't a comprehensive list of Satan's lies because he knows us and is aware of what will hurt us the most. It does provide an idea of a few of the ways in which Satan tries to discourage us. When he does attack us, we need to pray, asking for the presence of the Spirit to comfort and be with us, and then do as the scriptures suggests and, "Lift up your heads and receive the pleasing word of God, and feast upon his love; for ye may, if your minds are firm, forever" (Jacob 3:2).

Fighting a war against Satan in these latter days is not easy, but we are armed with the gift of the Holy Ghost and the love of a Heavenly Father who never leaves us comfortless and alone.

---

[34] Jennifer Nukols, "Truth and Lies," *Ensign,* October 200.(Bold type added by author.)

The Mantle of the Bishop

During the time that we were living in Illinois and attending the Litchfield Ward, changes were made to the bishopric. The most important one was the release of the current bishop and installing a new one. As usual, ward members were wondering who would be called and we were looking forward to knowing what would happen that day. When our new bishop stood to speak to us, it seemed like a typical first address to the congregation. He said he felt humbled by the new position he now held. He also jokingly asked us to "Be good, and make his job easier."

I was sitting with my family near the back of the chapel and could see almost the entire congregation in front of me. While the bishop was speaking, I saw one of my close friend's three-year-old son climb on the bench into a standing position. He seemed very excited and was pointing at the pulpit and saying something to his mother in a very animated way.

I was curious about what had caused all the commotion during the meeting, and after church when I passed my friend in the hall I asked her why her son was acting so agitated during Sacrament meeting. She said that he saw a cloak-like object descending down onto the bishop's shoulders as he spoke to us. Her son was pointing and asking his mother, "Do you see that? Do you see that?"

I know I didn't see anything, but a child doesn't make up this kind of story. He wasn't even old enough to know that with some callings a "mantle" falls upon the shoulders of those with special responsibilities in the church.

Elder Robert D. Hales asked this provocative question: "Have you ever wondered about this mantle which comes upon a bishop?" He explains, "There is something that happens to a man when he becomes a bishop because he learns more than anything else to honor the call."[35]

This mantle is mentioned in the scriptures in 2 Kings where we learn of the final act of Elijah. As the heavenly chariot carried him away, he dropped his cloak which Elisha later put on as he continued with the work of a prophet of God. He was able to perform wonders that confirmed to others that he truly was the Lord's designated servant. He wore the physical cloak that Elijah had worn and that had now been placed upon him (2 Kings 2:12-13).

In this same manner, but only figuratively, a mantle is placed upon bishops and others who are called to sacred positions in the church. Although this is not a physical piece of material, from my experience that day in church I have come to understand that it is nonetheless spiritually very real. Some few are actually able to witness the putting on of power and authority. I don't know if our bishop sensed something while he was addressing us, but I have always felt that the mantle of a bishop or any other priesthood holder is real, even though it is not usually visible with our physical eyes.

I have known the power of being set apart for many callings, including that of a full-time missionary. During the time of that service, my talents and faculties were enlarged. I was particularly aware of this when I was released from my mission to Northern California. I had become so accustomed to the feeling of sweet support that I

[35] Robert D. Hales, "The Mantle of a Bishop," *Ensign,* May 1985.

felt around me, that I was surprised when my stake president gave me a formal release and I suddenly felt those extra enhancements leave me. I walked around for days feeling a loss and realizing that I had been added upon during my service. I knew it was the power or mantle of the calling I held.

I have always tried to make sure that I am set apart for every calling that I receive. I know that my spiritual and temporal abilities are then maximized. I believe I am more able to magnify my stewardship after hands are laid upon my head during these priesthood blessings. It is such a miracle to have lay members of the Savior's church entrusted with His work and find that we are in many ways enlarged to enable us to better serve in this holy cause.

Pondering on the Piano Bench

Inspirational moments can come in the most intriguing and singular situations. One day while sitting on my piano bench, I was able to learn a little more about the true use of our talents and why the Lord gives them to us.

The revelation I received was precipitated by several events in my life. First, I had just moved into a very large and well-attended ward in Texas. This was a big change for me because our former ward was smaller and struggled for people who could serve. When new members moved there, they often were quickly called into leadership positions. While I was there I served as both Primary and Relief Society President.

As a result of serving so much and being so needed, I'm afraid I may have had an inflated view of my relative worth. Coming into this larger congregation was a bit of an adjustment for me because there were so many members who were capable, talented, and able to contribute to the work of the ward.

Transitions can be difficult and may take time to complete. For me life had become so altered that it created changes and challenges that I did not anticipate before I moved to the new location.

Then too, I think I was already feeling a little unimportant and wondering how the skills I had worked so diligently to developed might be helpful now. I have always had a strong desire to serve in the church.

One morning I had a few extra minutes, so I decided to practice the piano. I was sitting on the piano bench feeling like I was not as useful or needed as I wished I could be. I wanted to be able to do something. Then, I heard the Spirit gently ask me, "For what have your talents been given? Are they to bring you recognition and praise, or to serve the Lord and others?" This startling question only had one right answer; it was obvious. Then just like the Spirit often does, a gentle assurance followed: "You will be called upon when you are needed by the Lord."

What a miracle and an enlightening experience for me. I was able to have the voice of the Spirit remind me of the true purpose of gifts: "Seek ye earnestly the best gifts, always remembering for what they are given" (D&C 46:8). Clearly, we have these gifts so that we can bless others. I like this statement from Marianne Williamson, author of the book *A Return to Love*: "Success means we go to sleep at night knowing our talents and abilities were used in a way that served others."[36]

We should not wait until we feel we have big talents. I believe as Marianne Williamson suggests that "God can use the flimsiest résumé. He can use the smallest gifts. Whatever our gift is to God, however humble it may seem, He can turn it into a mighty work."[37] It is a blessing to not only have gifts and talents given to us, but also to have answers to our prayers. We are truly visited by the Lord and have the spirit of prophecy. Not only does the Lord know us, but He knows our talents, and will call upon us when they are needed.

It is also easy to envy others and wish that we had what they enjoy, along with our own abilities and aptitudes.

---

[36] Marianne Williamson, *A Return to Love* (New York City, New York: Harper Collins Publishers, 1992), 155.
[37] Ibid., 181.

Sometimes seeing so many talents among the ward members can cause me to feel jealous. One Sunday my Relief Society lesson dealt with the subject of the gifts of the Spirit. I wanted an object lesson that would help the sisters to have a clearer perspective on the use of our spiritual and temporal endowments.

I handed out several beautifully wrapped packages to a few sisters before Relief Society started. I explained that I would call on them during the lesson and ask if they would tell us what talents they had been given. I also let them know that sometime during the lesson someone would come and take their package.

Before the lesson I had prepared another sister to help me with the demonstration. I had given her a wrapped box and asked her to be prepared to tell us what special gifts she had in her life. I told her that I wanted her to take the packages of the other sisters, expressing her desire to have their gifts too.

During the course of my lesson, I asked each sister with a package to tell us what she thought her talents were. Then I called the other prepared sister. She explained what gifts the Lord had given her, and she also expressed how much she appreciated her gifts, but she wanted others. She got up and walked around the room, picking up the presents the sisters were holding and saying that she wanted all the things that they had been given. As she moved from sister to sister, the size of her pile grew larger and heavier. Soon it was so high, that she ended up dropping all of it on the floor.

One of the things that I hoped we all would remember was the principle in this scripture: "For all have not every gift given unto them; for there are many gifts, and to every man is given a gift by the Spirit of God. To some is given one, and to some is given another, that all may be profited there by" (D&C 46:11-12). Our gifts will bless others and ourselves if we use them correctly.

The Lord has not given each of us all the gifts available, but distributes them to different people so that we can all be edified and not overly distinguished or burdened with more than we can use to minister in the lives of others. As we learn in the Doctrine and Covenants: "Also the body hath need of every member, that all may be edified together" (D&C 84:110).

Pondering on the piano bench that day taught me many new and precious truths. What a tender and comforting miracle for me.

I Remember a Christmas

Christmas can be one of the most charming and cherished times of the year. It can also create challenges in our lives. With the decorating, the shopping, the gift wrapping, and the incoming family, there is often too much to do. One particular Christmas I learned how the Spirit can change, fix, and brighten any difficulty.

While we were living in Texas for the second time, we were in a house that was much larger than our previous home. This extra space was very exciting for our family because there were 8 of us living there at the time. It was fun and also an amazing adventure to not only live in a new home but also to be in a different area. Unfortunately, we had stretched ourselves financially to purchase the property, so we had to be careful about our expenditures.

With the advent of the upcoming holiday season, I discovered that not only did I not have enough decorations to deck the hall, but that the homes of my new friends were lavishly adorned. I decided that my decorations were dated and quite sparse in this setting. I agonized over this because I am not a decorator. I have often dreaded Christmas because "hanging the holly" is a prominent part of the holiday. First I have to take down everything currently decorating my rooms, and then I have to try to put up all new things. It is not only an enormous amount of work, but since it is not my forte, I did not look forward to this part of Christmas at any time, but this year was particularly stressful.

Then, a situation arose that caused "the squeeze" for me. My husband was the High Priest group leader and his Presidency had decided to have a Christmas party. He had volunteered our home without consulting me. Most of the time this is not advisable. Even though I love having parties, I had seen how people in my current, more prosperous neighborhood decorated for the season, and I felt quite inadequate in this situation.

One afternoon, I called on a sister and she invited me to come into her home and sit down to visit. Her rooms were so richly and resplendently decorated for Christmas that I felt even more troubled about holding the event. When I returned home, I walked around my house looking at each area and noticed how I had set out my ornaments. I just knew I couldn't have the party. That evening when my husband came home from work I said to him, "I don't want to have the party at our house. Let's have it at the church. Let's have it at someone else's house."

My husband wasn't sure how to handle my request because he knew how much I liked having people visit. First he tried to convince me to change my mind by explaining that we had enough room for the large group of High Priests and their wives that were planning to attend. Then, he also reminded me that the church was not available. "And besides," he insisted, "one's home is so much nicer during the holidays."

Then I tried to explain to him that I was uncomfortable by the sparse decorations and my inability to make it look gorgeous and glorious like the other houses I had seen. He attempted to reassure and comfort me. I just kept telling him, "I can't. I can't! "

He continued to say that it would be "Okay."

I was sure he didn't understand how I felt about the gathering even though I had tried to explain it to him. We were definitely in a stalemate situation.

Later that night I lay in bed wishing and praying that I wouldn't have to sponsor the evening—not here, not now. Then the Spirit whispered to me, "Just try." Just try? Well, yes, I could try. I didn't think it would turn out very well, but I could certainly try.

I began planning and then preparing for the party over the next few days. When the scheduled event arrived, the tables were set up with some seasonal centerpieces of pines, ribbons, and shimmering candles and they looked very lovely. Soon people began pouring in with their well-prepared dishes and expectations for a cozy and congenial Christmas evening. The food was delicious and the conversation was convivial. It reminded me of the scripture in the Doctrine and Covenants which says, "And that same sociality which exists among us here will exist among us there, only it will be coupled with eternal glory, which glory we do not now enjoy" (D&C 130:2). I am sure that the closeness we have with friends and family will be greater after this life, but the power of the Spirit can enhance any affair, even here on this sphere.

The Christmas spirit filled our home in abundance. Our friends were fun and interesting and my decorations didn't seem to matter. After a delectable dinner, we all trouped upstairs to our family room to share stories. We had chosen the theme, "I Remember a Christmas." Each person was to share a Christmas memory, either silly or serious. There were at least 30 people attending that night and our friends shared some of the funniest stories about Christmas that we have ever heard. We laughed and laughed, and it still is one of the most memorable and miraculous moments we have ever had in our home. I came to understand that if we just "try" our best, and serve, and listen to the Spirit, things will often turn out much better than we planned, or could have possibly anticipated.

As members of the church, we are often asked and reminded to pray for the influence of the Holy Ghost. On this particular holiday season I was able to learn first-hand one of the ways that the Spirit can enrich any occasion. Yes, I remember a Christmas!

An Issue with the Ivy

My little pot of ivy always sat so silently in its small container in the kitchen window, but it soon would speak volumes to me. Whenever I looked up and out onto the street, it felt so friendly, yet fragile. How I loved my little ivy. It added color and variety to my surroundings. It always managed to brighten my day.

Unfortunately, it was difficult to water because the window sill where it grew was across a large sink in the corner. Since providing the necessary moisture to help it thrive was not easy, I sometimes didn't do it. I thought it was not only too hard to reach, but I often felt that I was just too busy.

One morning I noticed my ivy looking a little forsaken. Instead of deciding to rededicate myself to its care, I remembered that I had some imitation ivy, and I thought I could add that to the pot until the plant revived. After the addition of the artificial ivy, the plant did look so much better.

Now I completely forgot to water it because it looked like it was flourishing. Week after week there was no visible change in the ivy. It never needed water, because it wasn't a real living thing. What I saw was synthetic.

Then one day while I was standing at my sink, I noticed my plant and realized I hadn't watered it for a long time. I strained over my sink to get it down from the ledge. I felt quite sad by what I found when I examined it more closely. I had let my little ivy die. It looked fine so I hadn't tended to it. The lack of care had caused it to wither away.

I spent some time thinking about the lesson I could learn from this issue with my ivy. What was I doing that just looked good but wasn't of true value? Was I filling my life with any counterfeit things that were choking out what might be better? Was I allowing what would be best to fade away by my choices? Was this a case of not actually prioritizing what I do every day?

Elder Dallin H. Oaks in his talk "Good, Better, Best" teaches this: "As we consider various choices, we should remember that it is not enough that something is good. Other choices are better, and still others are best. We have to forego some good things in order to choose others that are better or best because they develop faith in the Lord Jesus Christ and strengthen our families."[38]

The Lord clearly expects us to be proactive in our lives because he tells us "Men should be anxiously engaged in a good cause, and do many things of their own free will, and bring to pass much righteousness" (D&C 58:27). These principles are so important that they are highlighted in *For the Strength of Youth*: "You are also responsible for developing the talents and abilities Heavenly Father has given you. You are accountable to Him for what you do with your talents and how you spend your time. Choose to do many good things of your own free will."[39]

I try to remember the ivy when I make decisions about how to use the valuable resource of time and talents that I have been given. Without saying a word, the ivy taught me to fill my life with the very best that is available to me.

---

[38] Dallin H. Oaks, "Good, Better, Best." *Ensign,* November 2007.

[39] *For the Strength of the Youth* (Salt Lake City, Utah: The Church of Jesus Christ of Latter-day Saints, 2011), 3.

He Lifted Me

At a period in my life when six of my seven children were still at home, I often felt overwhelmed by the demands placed upon me. I was trying to clean and manage a large house, mostly by myself, and I also had several time-consuming church callings. I was an early morning seminary teacher, which required a great deal of preparation. I was also serving in the Stake Family History library. I had been called as the Activity Day Leader for the young girls in Primary. My daughter was part of that group; I loved working with them every week. I was trying to be a caring Visiting Teacher and also hoping to support my husband in his leadership calling. Sometimes I felt that I just couldn't do it all, and the weight of my responsibilities taxed me to the limit.

One night during this time, I had an extraordinary dream that changed my perspective. I dreamt that I was walking into the entrance of the church, and I saw a man several feet in front of me. He was higher than I was because the foyer was elevated by a one-step rise. I immediately recognized that this person was the Savior. One of the ways that I knew this was because He was dressed in a white robe. But more than what He was wearing and how He looked, I believe I discerned it spiritually. I walked up to Him, and He hoisted me high above His head. It wasn't what I expected, but it caused me to feel so loved and supported. This dream helped me as though it really happened.

Over the next few days when I thought about it, the part that stood out for me was that the Savior held up my entire body, all my weight, and it was not difficult for Him at all. In other words, it required no effort on His part to do that. For Him, supporting me was like lifting a feather. The cost of that effort has already been paid by the Savior through the Atonement. For a long time I felt like the Lord continued to help carry the weight of my laborious load.

After my dream, I was more fully able to understand Elder David A. Bednar words when he said, "Consider the Lord's uniquely individual invitation to 'take my yoke upon you.' Making and keeping sacred covenants yokes us to and with the Lord Jesus Christ. In essence, the Savior is beckoning us to rely upon and pull together with Him, even though our best efforts are not equal to and cannot be compared with His. As we trust in and pull our load with Him during the journey of mortality, truly His yoke is easy and His burden is light."

"We are not and never need be alone. We can press forward in our daily lives with heavenly help. Through the Savior's Atonement we can receive capacity and 'strength beyond [our] own' ('Lord, I Would Follow Thee,' Hymns, no. 220). As the Lord declared, 'Therefore, continue your journey and let your hearts rejoice; for behold, and lo, I am with you even unto the end' " (D&C 100:12).[40]

Sometimes I still try to do too much on my own and rely on the arm of flesh (2 Nephi 4:34). When I catch myself doing that I feel concerned because I know He wants to

---

[40] David A. Bednar, "Bear Up Their Burdens with Ease," *Ensign,* May 2014.

help me. I have taken His yoke upon me; and being yoked to the Savior, the Son of God, is one of the most incredible miracles that members of the church enjoy. We are promised again and again that He is always with us. I am still grateful to have been given a special dream one night that blessed me to know how it feels to be truly lifted by Him.

Counseling with the Lord

When one of my sons was in second grade, I was contacted by his teacher and asked to come to the school for a consultation regarding some of her concerns about him. I was unprepared for the conversation because I hadn't really expected him to be having any trouble. He was smart, sweet, and very obedient.

When I sat down with his teacher, she said that he seemed nervous and didn't really participate in discussions. Following this appointment, and after speaking with my husband, we decided to take our son to see a counselor that worked with our medical clinic. Unfortunately the hour we spent with this man was disturbing to my boy and very upsetting to me. The counselor seemed intent on laying blame on us as parents, and that hurt me deeply. It was all I could do to keep from crying as we left his office.

When I arrived at home I decided to do what always works best to comfort and direct me, and that is to petition the Lord for help. While I was praying, I flipped randomly through the pages of the Old Testament. I had been teaching it in seminary and was learning so much from the messages there. I found some verses that looked interesting, and so I stopped to read them. There on the page where I had paused was the word "counsel" in connection with the Lord (Judges 20:18). I read it and reread it. It was an answer for me.

I decided that if I could spend an entire hour with a complete stranger who knew nothing about me, my life, or my heart, I could also spend an hour each week with the

Lord. He knows everything about me, and I don't have to spend any time bringing him up to date on my problems. I began counseling almost immediately.

I already had a prayer journal, and now it began to be filled with the questions and answers that came because I was spending a complete hour each week talking to the Lord. As I continued to practice prolonged prayer, it became easier and more natural. Then I read in the Bible dictionary that, "As soon as we learn the true relationship in which we stand toward God, namely, God is our Father, and we are his children, then at once prayer becomes natural and instinctive on our part."[41]

Filling an hour became more of a discussion than having me do all the talking. I was explaining how I felt, what was taking place in my life, and what I hoped would happen. Then I would wait for answers. Soon I began to receive inspiration about where to look in the scriptures for help. I would read those verses and follow the entire scripture chain. I felt so blessed to have the many cross- references and scripture aids that are available in our standard works.

I developed a habit of counseling on Sunday morning before church. Even when our meetings started at 9:00 a.m., I always rose early enough to counsel for an hour. I began in 1994 and sometime after that, I felt instructed by the Spirit that this practice needed to be a permanent part of my life, and I knew that the Lord expected it of me. Weekly counseling was no longer optional.

We have been commanded to counsel. In Alma 37:37 we read, "Counsel with the Lord in all thy doings." Usually

[41] See "Prayer," Bible Dictionary, *The Holy Bible*, (Salt Lake City, Utah: The Church of Jesus Christ of Latter-day Saints, 1979), 752.

we reference this scripture to encourage us to pray about all things, but I think the word counsel means more than that. Now the Lord may just mean that we should talk to him about our lives and our decisions, but one of the definitions of counsel is, "Advice; instruction given in directing the judgement or conduct of another."[42] Shouldn't counseling then be more than just a one-sided conversation?

Young Women in the church are taught, "To counsel with the Lord is to discuss things with him. We tell him the desires and feelings of our hearts and then wait for an answer."[43]

When I began to spend longer with my counseling prayers, I didn't rush off. I listened for answers. Some came immediately and others came later. I always wrote down my question in the prayer journal, and then I left a space for an answer because I wanted to show my faith that I would receive one. D. L. Moody teaches, "If you pray for bread and bring no basket to carry it, you prove the doubting spirit, which may be the only hindrance to the boon you ask."[44]

The scriptures and the General Authorities talk a great deal about prayer and give us powerful guidance. I love some of the very specific suggestions that President Ezra Taft Benson has given to improve our communication with our Heavenly Father:

---

[42] The American College Dictionary, New York, Random House 1969 pg. 276.

[43] *Young Women's Manual 2, "Lesson 22:* Counseling with the Lord*"* (Salt Lake City, Utah: The Church of Jesus Christ of Latter-day Saints, 1993), 83-84.

[44] D. L. Moody, *http://www.azquotes.com/quote/545533*.

1. "**We should pray frequently**. We should be alone with our Heavenly Father at least two or three times each day: '… morning, mid-day, and evening,' as the scripture indicates (Alma 34:21.) In addition, we are told to pray always (2 Nephi 32:9; D&C 88:126). This means that our hearts should be full, drawn out in prayer unto our Heavenly Father continually" (Alma 34:27).

2. "**We should find an appropriate place where we meditate and pray**. We are admonished that this should be 'in your closets, and your secret places, and in your wilderness' (Alma 34:26). That is, it should be free from distraction, in secret" (3 Nephi 13:5–6).

3. "**We should prepare ourselves for prayer**. If we don't feel like praying, then we should pray until we do feel like praying. We should be humble (D&C 112:10). We should pray for forgiveness and mercy (Alma 34:17–18). We must forgive anyone against whom we have bad feelings (Mark 11:25). Yet, the scriptures warn, our prayers will be vain if we 'turn away the needy, and the naked, and visit not the sick and afflicted, and impart [not] of [our] substance.' (Alma 34:28).

4. "**Our prayers should be meaningful and pertinent.** We should not use the same phrases at each prayer. Each of us would become disturbed if a friend said the same few words to us each day, treated the conversation as a chore, and could

hardly wait to finish in order to turn on the TV and forget us."[45]

As I review these instructions from President Benson, it confirms that serious prayer isn't something easily done. I discovered that this kind of counseling needed careful planning. First of all, I always made sure that I had my prayer journal with me. I also brought a pen, my scriptures, a clock and a small note pad to collect random thoughts that occur while counseling. I found a spot where I would not be disturbed. I made sure I couldn't hear the phone ring. I found that conscientious preparations were very important.

Finding a peaceful place was very essential to counseling because I needed to be able to have enough quiet to maximize my ability to hear the still small voice. I know that the Holy Ghost can teach me anywhere, and at any time; but because my questions and His answers were so very vital to me, I needed to make sure that I was able to listen without any noise or distractions.

I know that sometimes more effort is needed to receive answers than just a quick one-minute prayer. I can't just kneel down and ask and expect everything to be laid out for me. Elder McConkie suggests that, "This mortality is a probationary estate. In it we have our agency. We are being tested to see how we will respond in various situations; how we will decide issues; what course we will pursue while we are here walking, not by sight, but by faith. Hence, we are to solve our own problems and then to

---

[45] Ezra Taft Benson, "Prayer," *Ensign*, May 1977. Bold type added by author.

counsel with the Lord in prayer and receive a spiritual confirmation that our decisions are correct."[46]

These thoughts by President Kimball express a similar idea: "Some things are best prayed over only in private, where time and confidentiality are not considerations...We hope that our people will have very bounteous prayers. It would not hurt us, either, if we paused at the end of our prayers to do some intense listening-even for a moment or two-always praying, as the savior did, 'not my will, but thine, be done.' (Luke 22:42)."

The problem that brought me to the exercise of counseling with the Lord started out as a difficult trial in my life. I didn't want to have to deal with another big concern with one of my children. After tackling previous problems concerning the other siblings, I wasn't sure I had the energy to cope with this. Thankfully, it became one of the sweetest, most inspiring, and helpful hardships I have ever had.

I have received so much help, inspiration, comfort, and direction from this practice that I cannot imagine how I would have survived the last 20 years without counseling with the Lord.

Some moments stand out from so many other moments by the sheer weight of our learning and the change of course that they create. This was one of those moments, one of my miraculous moments.

---

[46] Bruce R, McConkie, "Why the Lord Ordained Prayer," *Ensign*, January 1976.

The Dreaded Heart Attack

Our family's favorite activities on Family Home
Evening nights included anything athletic: hiking,
swimming, bike riding, or wall ball against the building
that was just outside our back gate.[47] Despite knowing this,
I still occasionally decided to take a chance on something
different. While looking for an idea for a church gathering
in *Big Ideas for Little Budgets*, I found a Heart Attack
activity and thought it would be outstanding for our family.
Essentially, it involves making hearts with messages of
love, support, and encouragement.[48]

My husband, Gary, and I agreed that we ought to heart
attack a sister in our ward who had recently been divorced
and was having both health and employment problems.
When we presented the idea to our children we were met
with the typical adolescent anguish and guttural groans—in
other words, a considerable amount of murmuring. Despite
their unenthusiastic response, we decided to proceed with
what we had planned.

After the opening prayer and song, the whole family
gathered around the kitchen table with red construction
paper, crayons, markers, and scissors. We each made a
heart and then wrote something on it that told the heart
attack recipient what we liked about her, how she was an
example to us, or what made her unique. During this part of

[47] See original publication: Gail H. Johnsen, "The Dreaded Heart
Attack," *Deseret News*, July 10, 2010.
[48] Brad Wilcox and John Bytheway, *Big Ideas for Little Budgets*
(Springville, Utah: Cedar Forts Publishing, 1995), 26.

the evening and also during the drive to the sister's home, the barrage of complaints continued.

When we arrived near our destination, we stealthy stopped down the street. While my husband stayed with the get-away car, the rest of the family piled out quickly and quietly, collectively sneaking to the front door with the pre-taped hearts. After each person fastened their message to the door, they began running toward the car. One brave soul rang the doorbell and then sprinted away to safety.

After we climbed into the van and the door had been closed, a collective cheer went up with comments like, "That was cool!" and "Can we do it again?" The children all wanted to know who else they could heart attack. The evening was fabulous and fun and everyone felt great about what we had done. We drove home feeling happy and satisfied, and then finished our evening with a closing prayer and treats.

While some of our Family Home Evenings did not turn out the way I hoped they would, occasionally we created something that ended up practically perfect.

For me it was a "And thus we see…" moment that I often find in the scriptures. It helped me to understand that I need to forge ahead with good ideas despite the occasional opposition, and let the experience of kindness and service create the joy for which they were intended.

My Day of Pentecost

Of all the stories I have told in *My Miraculous Moments*, this is by far the hardest to relate. I am sorely tempted to leave it out, but because the experience associated with this story was so unique for me and so powerful, I have decided to let all my warts show and just tell it like it really happened. My family will be acquainted with how I struggled through this situation and how I wanted to improve, but just wasn't able to do better than I did at that time.

Life is a journey, and I have discovered that I have so much to learn to be my best self. As Sister Lili Anderson teaches in her book, *Choosing Glory*, there is a "can't skip" principle in life. She says, "In order for our progress toward celestial life to be authentic and lasting, it must be built on the foundation of a terrestrial life. With very few exceptions, we progress step by step and cannot 'skip' from the telestial to the celestial realm."[49] As the scriptures so clearly teach, "For he will give unto the faithful line upon line, precept upon precept; and I will try you and prove you herewith" (D&C 98:12). I am hoping to grow and become a better person, and I have discovered that it doesn't happen in a day.

After we had lived in our ward in Texas for a few years, I had a misunderstanding with a sister. I stood back and judged her and felt that she was in the wrong, as we often

---

[49] Lili De Hoyos Anderson, *Choosing Glory* (Salt Lake City, Utah: These are the Great Days Publishing Company, LLC, 2009), 21.

do in these situations. Never mind the mote in my own eye! To make matters worse, I expected this woman to behave in a more charitable manner than she did. I thought that because her husband was prominent in his career and their family was very well-to-do, and also because they had a large family of talented children who were often up in front of the ward performing, that she should behave in a certain way: the way "I" thought she should act under the circumstances. One can easily see that I was in the wrong here, and obviously just jealous from the beginning of this event. Perhaps I am not alone in sometimes feeling envious of others. Ralph Waldo Emerson once said that "Envy is the tax which all distinction must pay."[50] If we stand out in exceptional ways from others, jealousy may sometimes occur.

Not long after this unsettling event occurred with the ward member, I was attending Sacrament meeting and learned that our bishop was being released. It was unexpected. Then the new bishop was called. To my dismay and shock it was this women's husband. Somehow I got through the three-hour meeting block, but when I arrived at home, the dam definitely burst. I went into my bedroom, locked the door, and then I went into my bathroom and locked that door. I went to the back of my bathroom and sobbed. I took a towel to cover my face so that no one in my family would hear me. I cried and cried because now this family was going to be more distinguished and visible than before. I didn't think I could stand it.

---

[50] William H Gilman, ed., *The Journals and Miscellaneous Notebooks of Ralph Waldo Emerson: Vol. II 1822-1826* (Cambridge, Mass.: The Belknap Press of Harvard University Press, 1961), 202.

Finally I calmed down enough to pray. I told the Lord, who was already well aware of my feelings—having shared them on many occasions—that I just didn't know how I could live with it. I really felt strongly about my low tolerance level. I had this conversation with the Lord, and as I poured out my heart, I began to feel it soften a little. I truly wanted to want what He wanted. I was sure that those in authority were inspired, and that obviously this was the Lord's choice. When I realized that, I decided I needed to get myself into the right place. There was only one right side here, and that was on the Lord's side.

I also assured the Lord that since this was who He wanted to be our bishop I was going to support His decision with all my heart and soul. I told Him: "No matter how hard this is for me, I will absolutely sustain this man."

Suddenly, I heard a rushing wind, and it blew into my bathroom. It was exactly like the manifestation described in the scriptures at the day of Pentecost (Acts 2:2). I felt it gust over me and then pass out of that small space. At first I was confounded, and then comforted. Although I wasn't able to speak in tongues which occurred on that other day, I can truly say that I was amazed. I knew the story from the scriptures very well but didn't realize that it was something that might happen today. Now I believe that the ways in which the Holy Ghost can manifest Himself are many and varied. The gift I was given that day was to be able to sustain my leaders.

I love these thoughts by George Albert Smith, 8th President of the Church: "There is only one pathway of safety for me in this day and that is to follow those whom the Lord has appointed to lead. I may have my own ideas and opinions, I may set up my own judgment with reference to things, but I know that when my judgment conflicts with the teachings of those that the Lord has given to us to point the way, I should change my course. If I desire salvation I will follow the leaders that our Heavenly Father has given to us, as long as he sustains them."[51]

Both President Smith and President James E. Faust agree on the correct course of safety for the saints. Elder Faust has said, "In my lifetime, there have been very few occasions when I questioned the wisdom and inspiration given by key priesthood leaders. I have always tried to follow their counsel, whether I agreed with it or not. I have come to know that most of the time they were in tune with the Spirit and I was not. The safe course is to sustain our priesthood leaders and let God judge their actions."[52]

It is easier for me to sustain my leaders now that I understand that the Lord expects me to trust the workings of the church even though I know that the people who are called into positions are not perfect. It also seems truly remarkable to me that the Lord will allow us our agency to sustain and support those that He calls. I discovered that day that when we deliberately choose to follow the Lord and his leaders, He knows.

---

[51] *Teachings of Presidents of the Church: George Albert Smith* (Salt Lake City, Utah: The Church of Jesus Christ of Latter-day Saints, 2011), 61.

[52] James E. Faust, "Power of the Priesthood," *Ensign*, May 1997.

Sugar Blues

During junior high school I began a trend that would take me through many years of my life: dieting. I would gain a few pounds, diet them off, put them back on, and start the entire process over again. It became a way of life, but it bothered me. I prayed about it, asking for help, and that often led me to books and information that were helpful. A more healthy eating style was what I really needed.

Finally in my early forties, when I was counseling regularly on Sunday mornings and spending enough prayer time to really ask and listen, I prayed about my dieting and weight again. I felt like desserts were a major culprit in the struggle, and I was talking to the Lord about how I equated "food" with "fun." I thought that the connection between those two were pretty legitimate for me in my family and also from a social standpoint.

My mother was a great cook and food was part of every event, as it usually is with any party or gathering. I wanted to separate food from fun though, and tried to reframe my thinking so that I could enjoy activities without a sugary treat. I wasn't having much success on my own, however.

I counseled about it one Sabbath and when I was in my listening and pondering phase, the title of a book came clearly into my mind. The name of the book was *Sugar Blues* by William Duffy.[53] I hadn't heard anyone mention that title for 15 years, but there it was front and center in

---

[53] William Duffy, *Sugar Blues* (New York City, New York: Warner Books Inc., 1975).

my mind. Since I always had my prayer journal page divided into two parts: first, the place where I would write questions, and then the place where I would put the answer/assignment, I wrote down *Sugar Blues* and bought it that week. I read it pretty quickly and felt more than ever that I needed to take sugar out of my diet. Today, there are lots of books, articles, and information on the internet about sugar, but I only knew of that one book at the time.

I had asked the Lord what to do, and he had told me to read that book. I felt that I needed to follow my impression about sugar. I have noticed that the words in the sacrament prayer are that we "Keep his commandments which he has given them" (D&C 20:77). I believe that He means the large commandments, and also those directions that are individual to me. I knew that I had been given personal instruction and guidance that the Lord now expected me to follow.

Heavenly Father is very merciful. We may pray endlessly about our problems, but I feel that He doesn't always give us all the information and resources we desire until He knows that we have the strength, the maturity, and the knowledge to follow what He wants us to do. Once we know something, really know it I mean, then we are responsible to the Lord for that information.

I had followed the pattern of studying a topic out in my mind, making a decision, and then praying about it (D&C 9:8). I had received an answer and I knew what I had to do. I had to stop eating desserts and start paying more attention to the labels on everything I bought.

It seemed like something I could do! I was very optimistic about being able to handle this assignment. But, unfortunately, there truly is opposition in all things (2

Nephi 2:15). Almost anytime I begin to improve myself in any way, for example setting a goal to be more patient, gracious, or kind, I encounter roadblocks which act as a check to see if I really am determined to accomplish my objective.

Several days after making my decision not to eat sugar, it was Halloween! My children went out in the neighborhood and brought home bags of candy. Then they carefully sorted everything into piles. There was always something in their stash that they didn't like and would share with me if I asked. I didn't eat much, but I did eat some of it.

On the morning of November 1st, I woke up and I knew that I was in trouble. I wish I could describe the feeling more clearly. It wasn't like a dark cloud over me, but I felt a divine disapproval. It was familiar because I had felt it once before. On one occasion, I had prayed for something amiss, and had felt the exact same feeling (2 Nephi 4:35). I quickly withdrew my request at that time and afterwards was more careful about my petitions in the future.

But suddenly the morning after Halloween there it was again! It was a loving correction—I didn't feel judged but knew I had acted against the Lord's counsel. How does the Lord express his divine disapproval and yet still cause me to feel so loved? When others try to correct or criticize me, I feel hurt and unhappy. When the Holy Ghost teaches me how to alter my path I feel nurtured and loved. Perhaps, a key to this is found in the book, *The Better People Leader*. The author teaches, "When done kindly, objectively, and straightforwardly, even receiving negative feedback can be considered a positive experience."[54]

I haven't had desserts for many decades and quite often I am asked why I don't. It's a little awkward to explain quickly. I can't really say that I gave up sugar completely, because sugar is in practically everything we eat, even ketchup. But I do avoid it as much as possible, and I feel blessed both spiritually and physically for that decision.

Knowing how harmful it really is to our bodies, and yet seeing it put into so many foods that we eat every day, always makes me think of the words in the Doctrine and Covenants. The Lord says, "In consequence of the evils and designs which do and will exist in the hearts of conspiring men in the last days, I have warned you, and forewarned you, by giving unto you the word of wisdom by revelation" (D&C 89:4).

I realize that the Word of Wisdom does not restrict us from eating sugar. I'm not saying that it does. But the Lord is interested in our bodies, and wants us to do everything we can to take care of them. The Doctrine and Covenants teaches that this principle is "adapted to the capacity of the weak and the weakest of all saints, who are or can be called saints." Perhaps we might individually hold ourselves to the highest standards of health that we can. Of course, we have to decide for ourselves just what that will entail.

I don't try to force this non-sugar habit on my family. They have to come to their own decision about how to live their lives. I just know that for me, when the Lord gives me direction, I need to follow it.

---

[54] Charles A. Coonradt, *The Better People Leader* (Layton, Utah: Gibbs Smith Publisher, 2007), 86.

The Prophet Speaks to Me

Most people don't even know where the island of Guam is located even though it is one of the five United States territories. Flying west from Los Angeles, it takes about seven hours to get to Hawaii, and then from there it is another seven or eight hours to arrive in Guam. Or there is a flight through Japan. With either choice, it's a long way from Texas. We moved to Guam for my husband's job with Exxon. My three oldest children were in college and one was serving a mission; we only brought our three youngest with us.

Being in Guam was a challenge for me in many ways. Shortly after we moved there, Exxon was required by the FTC to sell their assets as a condition of the merger with Mobil, and we knew that we would only be temporary residence on the island. We did not know, however, how long we would live on that faraway, tropical paradise. Month after month we were told that a decision would come shortly. Living in this somewhat transient situation has never been my strong suit.

Another one of my problems was my teenage daughter, Jocelyn, who had been diagnosed with mononucleosis the summer before we moved to Guam. She was not herself the entire time we lived there. She had to change from the high school where she started in the fall to another school because she was not able to keep up with the stringent curriculum. A member of the church suggested we go to the Catholic school where her daughter attended, but shortly after we registered there, she changed schools. We didn't feel like we could move Jocelyn again, so we left her there. It was very difficult for all of us. Even the nuns were unhappy because she often questioned their teachings using her knowledge of our LDS doctrine to explain what she knew to be true.

In addition to these other concerns, for the first time in their lives, my children found out what it felt like to be in the minority. Residents on the island included people from many locations on the globe, but the Chamorro people are the natives there and the largest group. These and other factors made our adjustment even more challenging.

One of the things we appreciated while we were there was the chance to able to serve in the Talisay branch of the church. This was perhaps my favorite part the assignment. I enjoyed getting to know the people who lived there and serving with them. Unfortunately this was not enough to offset the hardships we faced during that time.

Eventually the sale of the Exxon properties occurred, and the arrangements for our family's future were completed. We began planning our move back to Texas. In February 2000, before we left the island, we heard that President Hinckley was going to be in Guam while his plane was being refueled before it continued on to his next stop. He had decided to come and speak to the members on the island. We were all very excited.

When we arrived at the location for the meeting with President Hinckley, we saw that the room provided for the evening was large, but not the size of an auditorium by any means. Our family was seated as far back as you could be on the speaker's left side, but we could still clearly see President and Sister Hinckley. Since we were on the last row, I sat a bit higher in my seat and strained a little to get a better view.

I wasn't praying or asking for any specific instruction, and so I felt blessed to have the heavenly gift that I was given. During his talk, President Hinckley began speaking about the people who had come to Guam. He mentioned how few members there were when he came before on a previous visit, and how we now filled up the room. He was thanking people for coming to Guam: the young elders and sisters, the older missionaries, the military people, and others for taking the opportunity to be on the island. Then he just turned his head in our direction and said: "Thank you for coming to Guam." It seemed like he was looking directly at me. It felt like the Lord was personally thanking me for the sacrifice I had made in coming there, and for my obedience in following the Spirit. It was a wonderful sensation.

The thing that had sustained me throughout the ordeal was a clear directive from the Spirit that I had received earlier. One day while we were living in Texas, my husband came home from work and told me that he had been asked whether he wanted to throw his hat in the ring for a job in Guam. We had several serious conversations about it and finally decided to agree to be available. Then we prayed about that decision. I received a very clear impression that we should say we would take the transfer if it was offered to us.

After that we said prayers along the way about going, but I never received any other inspiration or direction than the original one that I had been given. The Lord, in His economy, answered my first prayer, and that was all I received.

We were glad that we had gone to Guam because we learned a great deal from living there. But it was a sacrifice in many ways. Being able to remember that I had received a confirmation to my decision to go to Guam was always the foundation that supported me in the troubles I faced.

The scriptures provide a basis for such sacrifices through the theology provided by such words: "And every one that hath forsaken houses, or brethren, or sisters, or father, or mother, or wife, or children, or lands, for my name's sake, shall receive an hundredfold, and shall inherit everlasting life" (Matthew 19:29). I have a testimony that the Lord will compensate me and all of His children for all we endure in righteousness.

Shortly before we left the island, I had this ratification with the visit of President Hinckley and of receiving a "thank you." I knew that the Lord was telling me that I had made the right decision to come, and that He knew I had followed His direction even though it was difficult. I know that I can count on these blessings coming in the Lord's time.

President N. Eldon Tanner asked this profound question: "How long has it been since you made a sacrifice for someone or for some good cause?" Then he continues by saying this, "Remember that sacrifice brings forth the blessings of heaven. Remember also that the things of greatest worth to us today—our membership in the Church, the knowledge we have of God and his son, Jesus Christ, the plan of life and salvation, the bounties of the earth, the standards of living we enjoy—were all obtain through the sacrifice of man."[55]

---

[55] N. Eldon Tanner, "Sacrifice," *Ensign,* June 1981.

Sometimes I feel that when the Lord desires to enrich my life, He provides opportunities for me to forfeit something that I value. If I take advantage of the chances that are offered, I find that I have grown in both learning and spirituality. What I gained in Guam far exceeded what I had to give up to be there. This law of sacrifice that the Lord provides for us can be a living miracle in our lives. I really do believe this is true!

Will They Remember Me?

When members of the church move to Guam they often bring with them a great deal of gospel knowledge and experience. For this reason many are called to leadership positions and asked to serve in a variety of ways, sacrificing a larger amount of time in building up the church.

One Sunday I had a brief conversation with one of the women in my branch who, like me, also was not a native of Guam. She rhetorically mused about the service she had given while she was there and wondered out loud, "Will these people remember me?" It was a very interesting question, and provided me with the opportunity to ponder on the results of my service. I thought about it for several days and asked myself if I would be remembered, and also, if I cared.

I decided first of all, that no, I probably would not be remembered. Many members come and go on the island, and I was just one of them. They might remember who I was if I came back, but not what particular work I had done there. For me the most important part of the question was, "Am I doing this to be remembered?" The answer again was no.

What I decided, after a fair amount of contemplation, was that I hoped to have them remember the Savior. I asked myself, "Have I stepped aside sufficiently and pointed them in the direction of the most eminent and exemplary person I know?"

We are commanded many times in the scriptures to remember, and we know that this is an important gospel principle. What are we to remember though? It is to daily recall our covenants and promises to Father in Heaven and the Savior as the means that supplies us with the surest and safest avenue of success in our lives. Remembering me wouldn't help them. Remembering the Savior would.

In the Book of Mormon, the words in Moroni ring true to me, because we are told to "Come unto Christ" (Moroni 10:32). Helping others to come unto Christ will give them a better foundation of help, healing, and the kind of a hero than neither I, nor anyone else I know, can possibly provide. If they look to me, I am going to disappoint them sooner or later, but the Savior never will.

Elder Jeffrey R Holland testified that: "The soul that comes unto Christ dwells within a personal fortress, a veritable palace of perfect peace…This is my basic message to each of you, wherever you live, whatever your joys or sorrows, however young or old you may be, at whatever point you may find yourself in this mortal journey of ours…I offer you, 'the way…the life' (John 14:6). Wherever else you think you may be going, I ask you to 'come unto him' as the imperative first step in getting there, in finding your individual happiness and strength and success."

"Whoever we are and whatever our problems, his response is always the same, forever. 'Come unto me. Come and see what I do and how I spend my time. Learn of me, follow me, and in the process I will give you answers to your prayers and rest to your souls' "[56]

The question this sister asked sparked in me an internal journey regarding the purpose and plan of the work that I had been doing my whole life. It helped me to realize that I really only had one calling in the church no matter where I served, and that was to invite others to "Come unto Christ."

---

[56] Jeffrey R. Holland, "Come Unto Me," *Ensign*, April 1998 (adapted from a CES Young Adult Fireside given on March 2,1997 at Brigham Young University).

The Parable of the Popcorn Ball

The Young Women in our ward were planning an activity, and I was asked to bring a dessert.[57] I chose popcorn balls. After popping the corn and separating the popped from the unpopped kernels, I placed the popcorn in a dish that would make it convenient for stirring in the syrup. Then I proceeded to make that mixture and added a color to make them more attractive.

During the day, I had been thinking and praying about a particular blessing that I was seeking from the Lord. I was pleading earnestly for His help in obtaining this favor and was actually feeling that I had somehow been left behind. It was almost as if I needed to be given what I wanted now or the Lord would run out of blessings and I would miss out completely.

As I poured the syrup over the popcorn and began to stir the ingredients together, my youngest daughter, Karen, came into the room. She saw that I was making popcorn balls and was disappointed when she learned that they were not for our family, but for someone else.

"Can I have one?" she asked.

"I'll have to see if I have enough" was my immediate response to her question.

She waited somewhat impatiently and was encouraging me to make the popcorn balls smaller so the likelihood that she would get one would increase. She was in and out of

---

[57] See original publication: Gail H. Johnsen, "Popcorn Ball Forms Parable for Mother," *Deseret News*, February 14, 2009.

the kitchen several times to check on my progress and the probability of getting a popcorn ball.

After about her third entrance into the kitchen, and additional amounts of concern about whether there would be enough for her, I suddenly realized that she had nothing to worry about.

"I am the popcorn ball maker," I told her. "There is no shortage here, and I can make another batch, if I need to do so. Don't worry; you will get a popcorn ball."

Suddenly, I understood that the Lord was trying to teach me an important lesson. I remembered that in the scriptures, the Lord had been called our "Maker." In Enos, we read: "And my soul hungered; and I kneeled down before my Maker, and I cried unto him in mighty prayer and supplication for mine own soul; and all the day long I did cry unto him; yea, and when the night came I did still raise my voice high that it reached the heavens" (Enos 1:4).

My Heavenly Father had not only heard my prayer that day but had found a way to teach me through everyday events that He truly is the "Maker" and that He has no shortage of ingredients to supply me with the blessing for which I was pleading as my voice reached high into the heavens. He knows what we need and when we need it—and will provide for us according to His will and His perfect timing.

Becoming Like the Savior

One morning I awoke full of anticipation because of my upcoming trip to see family in Utah.[58] I had a long list of things to do before I left, but I knew I had time to do all of them if I organized myself. Unfortunately, when my husband went out to the garage to go to work, he discovered that my car had a flat tire. He quickly inflated it enough to get me to a repair shop and then left for work.

It took me until midmorning to get packed and ready enough so that I could get my tire fixed. Even though I wasn't first in line at the repair shop, they told me it would only take an hour, so I shopped in a department store while I waited.

After an hour I returned and was promised it would only be another 30 minutes. "OK," I thought, "I can deal with this."

When another 30 minutes were over, I went back. A new employee was there, and he said that it would be "Another 30 minutes." Now I started to feel upset, and a little pinched for time.

I decided to exhibit some patience and long-suffering, so I continued to wait. But since I had an early afternoon flight I knew I couldn't delay much longer if I was going to be on time to the airport. I started mentally crossing things off my list because I knew I would not have time to do them now.

During this 30 minutes, however, I started to watch my car and I saw that it was not getting any closer to being

---

[58] See original publication: Gail H. Johnsen, "About Becoming Like Christ," *Deseret News*, Dec. 26, 2011.

serviced, and that it was by no means going to be only another 30 minutes. Now I was frustrated, anxious, and felt like they were lying to me. I wanted to go and tell them what I thought about their "30 minutes."

Instead of expressing my frustration in a loud voice or with threats, I decided to tell the attendant my situation. My car was immediately driven into the garage and the tire was repaired. I slashed almost everything off my list and rushed home to get my suitcases before continuing on to the airport.

Later that day, while waiting to board the plane, I sat quietly thinking about how much energy and strength it had taken not to yell at someone. That would have been easy; being patient, showing kindness, and displaying long-suffering were hard. Then I thought, "Heavenly Father, I hope you have a big reward for me for the way I handled this one!" And in His loving and patient wisdom He opened a little window for me. The Spirit whispered that it wasn't about rewards; it was about becoming like Heavenly Father and His Son.

At the end of my life, the Lord isn't going to drive up with either a small station wagon or a large semi-truck filled with various prizes all neatly wrapped just for me. What He wants is that each one of us become like He is. I suddenly understood the progression of knowing, doing, and finally becoming.

Elder Dallin H. Oaks of the Quorum of the Twelve expresses the thought in this way, "As important as it is to lose every desire for sin, eternal life requires more. To achieve our eternal destiny, we will desire and work for the qualities required *to become* an eternal being."[59]

I am grateful for this unusual challenge, the life lesson given to me, and especially for the words of an apostle that reinforced what I learned.

---

[59] Dallin H. Oaks, "Desire," *Ensign,* May 2011. (Italic added by author.)

The Choir Sings Again

While living in Texas, our stake was scheduled to have a General Authority visit us. On that Sabbath, I was participating in the choir which was filled with many talented singers. We had practiced longer and harder than usual because of our guest. But during the meeting we had the opportunity to enjoy a unique musical moment together. I already knew the power that sacred music can have on the message and spirit of the meeting, but I could not have anticipated the beautiful experience that we as a choir would share.

That Sunday everything proceeded as scheduled with the stake presidency's welcome, the opening song, and the invocation. There were several speakers and then it was the choir's turn to participate. We rose from our seats and the organ began. Our director raised her arms to lead us in singing the song that we knew so well. I was just trying to perform in the same way that I had practiced, but for some reason I couldn't produce the volume that I wanted. It felt as if my voice was being held back. I continued to participate, but wondered if there was something the matter with me or my vocal instrument. Since this had never happened to me before, I felt frustrated and confused.

After the members of the stake presidency spoke, the General Authority began his remarks. He talked for a few minutes and then stopped. He looked back at the choir and did something that seemed unusual to me. He asked us to sing that same number again. I glanced around and saw the puzzled looks on the faces of the other members of our group.

The choir director took her place and motioned for us to rise. We all stood to sing. This performance was different though. It felt like my voice and the voices around me were released, and we just sounded amazing. The intensity was impressive, and it filled the entire room. I had all the volume that I could possibly muster. When we sat down, the General Authority made a comment about how the choir had been magnified during the reprise. He said that it was so much better, and that it was almost like angels had attended us.

I have heard of angel choirs from the scriptures; angels came to herald the Savior's birth. I had been told by a friend that angels sang with earthly choirs at a funeral she had attended for a little baby girl, but I have never known if I had been part of a choir joined with heavenly singers. I don't know if angels sang with us, but we definitely were enlarged with the second presentation. It felt as if heaven and earth joined together for a few minutes to praise our Heavenly Father and bear testimony through music.

I believe in the majesty of music and know that it can transcend this lower realm. I also know that there is definitely a Celestial place where music is beyond our understanding. Elder Callister reminds us that, "If we could peek behind the heavenly veil, we would likely be inspired by the music of heaven, which is probably more glorious than any music we have heard on this earth.[60]

---

[60] Douglas L. Callister, "Our Refined Heavenly Home" (Devotional Address, Brigham Young University, September 19, 2002).

Music is a gift from heaven and blesses and lifts us. President Brigham Young once said, "There is no music in hell, for all good music belongs to heaven. It would be punishment enough to go to hell and not hear a note of music for eternity.[61]

This statement in *For the Strength of Youth* relates to all members no matter what their age: "Music has a profound effect on your mind, spirit, and behavior." Then it continues: "Choose carefully the music you listen to. Pay attention to how you feel when you are listening. Some music can carry evil and destructive messages. Do not listen to music that encourages immorality or glorifies violence through its lyrics, beat, or intensity. Do not listen to music that uses vulgar or offensive language or promotes evil practices. Such music can dull your spiritual sensitivity."[62]

Not only is good music miraculous, but it can also have a bad influence on us. President Thomas S. Monson said: "Music can help you draw closer to your Heavenly Father. It can be used to educate, edify, inspire, and unite. However, music can, by its tempo, beat, intensity, and lyrics, dull your spiritual sensitivity. You cannot afford to fill your minds with unworthy music."[63]

---

[61] Excerpt from Brigham Young's dedication of a new theater in Salt Lake City on March 6, 1862, as quoted by Rulon T. Burton, *We Believe* (Salt Lake City, Utah: Tabernacle Books, 1994), 598.

[62] *For the Strength of Youth* (Salt Lake City, Utah: The Church of Jesus Christ of Latter-day Saints, 2011), 22.

[63] Thomas S. Monson, "Preparation Brings Blessings," *Ensign*, May 2010.

Sister Rosemary Wixom shared these insights: "Your choice of music can also affect your ability to accomplish tasks or to learn. Two researchers explored this relationship by studying the effects of music and rhythm on the nervous system of mice. For eight weeks, one group of mice constantly listened to Strauss waltzes (highly organized and orderly music), while a second group heard disharmonious sounds in the form of continuous drumbeats. A third group was raised in silence.

"After eight weeks, the mice were placed in a maze to find food. The mice in the second group wandered off with no sense of direction—"a clear indication they were having trouble learning"—and took much longer to find the food than they had at the beginning of the study. The mice exposed "to discordant sounds not only developed difficulties in learning and memory...but they also incurred structural changes in their brain cells." The researchers' diagnosis is very interesting: "We believe that the mice were trying to compensate for this constant bombardment of disharmonic noise...They were struggling against the chaos."[64]

What could be the "chaos" in some of today's music— things that might keep us from learning effectively? It may relate to the rhythm and beat of the music (as with the mice) or with the words used or messages presented. President Boyd K. Packer, President of the Quorum of the Twelve Apostles, said: "We are living at a time when society is undergoing a subtle, but powerful, change. It is becoming more and more permissive in what it will accept in its entertainment. As a result, much of the music being

---

[64] Rosemary M. Wixom, "The Influence of Music," *New Era*, September 2013.

performed by popular entertainers today seems to be more intended to agitate than to pacify, more to excite than to calm."[65]

One of my favorite callings in the church was as the Ward Music Leader. I have seen how spiritual music can affect our meetings, so I tried diligently to make sure that we had special musical numbers whenever we had an available Sunday. I always noticed that after the musical interlude the Spirit in the room seemed stronger. Then, I like to say a silent prayer of gratitude for the performer who had to sacrifice so much time and effort to be able to provide the inspiring performance. I also feel grateful to the lyrists and the composers who shared their gifts in this way. I feel especially thankful to Heavenly Father for providing our world with so many glorious melodies.

Some of the most important and beloved music we have in the church comes from the Children's Song Book. Many of these songs stay with us when our Primary lessons may have been forgotten. One of my favorite stories about the influence of Primary music came from a sister in my ward whose son attended a military academy. While he was exercising in the gym he often heard the other cadets sharing sexually-oriented stories and using vulgar language. He soon realized that if he sang Primary songs in his mind, he could distract himself from what was being said. It was a huge help to be able to pull out those lyrics and melodies in a moment.

When we listen to spiritual music we can feel transported by what we hear and by what we experience whether it is

---

[65] Boyd K. Packer, "Worthy Music, Worthy Thought," *Liahona*, April 2008.

our church hymns or other compositions that are available to us. What a miracle our choir enjoyed that day and what a blessing music produces in our lives.

The Sunday School Lesson

One Sunday I was in Salt Lake City attending my sister's ward, and listening to the Gospel Doctrine lesson and discussion on the assigned topic. It was something about how to raise a righteous family. During the lesson, a young father made a comment that suggested that if we take our children to Sacrament and our other meetings, have scripture study, and family prayer that they would all stay in the church, and everything would turn out okay.

I was feeling very hurt, somewhat cynical, and probably a little bit bitter about my family. I hoped that I had done everything I was capable of doing to teach my children the gospel. I had been diligent in having Family Home Evenings, sometimes even two a week. We had one on Sunday with a spiritual lesson and one on Monday for a fun, family activity. We read the scriptures as a family almost every morning and had family prayer. We tried to kneel down at night to pray together.

We took our children to church and made sure that we kept the Sabbath day holy whether we were on vacation or visiting family. We always shopped on Saturday to make sure we didn't have to buy food or other supplies on the Sabbath. I had listened to the counsel of the brethren and had tried faithfully to follow it. Unfortunately, parenting is always a matter of two imperfect people raising children in a telestial world. And no matter how hard we try to teach our children the gospel, they have their agency. Several of them had fallen away from the church and the gospel, and it was really difficult to understand and to endure.

I heard this young father express his feelings that the prescribed effort would bring about the desired results and bursting forth from my hurting heart I thought, "Right!" I had seen for myself that it didn't always turn out that way. Then into my mind came the clear and unmistakable voice of the Spirit reminding me that "I the Lord, am bound when you do what I say" (D&C 82:10). I knew that because I had done everything in my power to raise my children the way the Lord expected me to do it, that I had bound Him to bless me and my family. Maybe the young father was right; it may not turn out exactly the way I anticipated when I started, but the Lord would forever be mindful of my family because He promised He would.

I know that many parents understand this feeling of bitterness, disappointment, and surprise when after doing everything in their power to raise their families in righteousness they find them falling away from the Lord's plan of happiness. Even the Lamanites who were converted to the Lord began to lose faith when the same thing happened to them. "And there was also a cause of much sorrow among the Lamanites; for behold, they had many children who did grow up and began to wax strong in years, that they became for themselves, and were led away by some who were Zoramites by their lying and their flattering words, to join those Gadianton robbers. And thus were the Lamanites afflicted also, and began to decrease as to their faith and righteousness, because of the wickedness of the rising generation" (3 Nephi 1:29-30).

Although I may doubt at times that I have really done all I could do, or wonder if I truly taught my family sufficiently, I believe that in the end, I can only work out my own salvation and that everything that happens to me will be to test my faith and to help increase my testimony and my conviction in following the Savior. This is really my most important responsibility. I must make sure that I don't lose faith and falter or fail to keep my own covenants.

Elder Cook encourages us with these words: "Brothers and sisters, if we faithfully have family prayer, scripture study, family home evening, priesthood blessings, and Sabbath day observance, our children will...be prepared for an eternal home in heaven, regardless of what befalls them in a difficult world."[66] This statement gives me hope that the work I have done here has prepared my children for heaven.

Since I was where I was supposed to be on that Sunday morning even though I was on vacation, the Lord took the hurt and disappointment out of my heart by reassuring me through the Spirit that He can heal and help at any time.

What a miracle we enjoy as members of the church. We are surrounded by good teachers, and also a member of the Godhead who speaks to us while we are being taught in classes or during scripture study. He can reach down into our hearts and answer our questions and address our fears. The Lord wants us to bind Him so that we can receive our promised inheritance. He tells us that the way to do this is to do what He says, keep the commandments.

---

[66] Quentin L. Cook, "The Lord Is My Light," *Ensign*, May 2015.

Look!

My son, Zane, and I started out early one summer morning for our marathon drive to Utah. It was challenging, but we always chose to drive straight through from Houston to Salt Lake City. It was an exhausting 24-hour drive, but with two of us it was easier.

We were taking turns at the wheel and had finally gotten past the midway mark in our journey, which is usually somewhere in New Mexico. I was driving and noticed that I only had about one-fourth tank of gas left. It was almost midnight and I thought perhaps I ought to stop at the next town because from 12 to 6 in the morning open gas stations are less frequent in that area. I decided filling up my gas tank would be a good decision at that late hour.

As I drove through a small town, I saw a well-lit gas station, and it seemed to have customers, so I pulled in. A young man who was hosing off the driveway came over and told me that their station was closed, but I could get gas across the street. I looked over at that gas station and the whole place looked deserted. Nevertheless, I believed him.

I pulled across the street and up to the pump. There was not a single person there, and no lights were illuminating the service center. As soon as I stopped the car, Zane jumped out and went to the pump to get some gas. Before he could even slide our credit card through the reader to pay for our purchase, two young teenage boys drove up and got out of their car. They told my son that they needed gas but didn't have a credit card. They asked if they could give him $10 and use our card. Zane walked back to the driver's side where I was sitting and started talking to me about it.

I had hardly looked up since I had stopped the car. I was busy straightening up the seats and putting wrappers and other miscellaneous items in a garbage sack that I kept handy. Suddenly, I felt a strong impression that seemed to command, "Look!" I glanced up and found that there were two other cars there besides the boy's vehicle. One was a large van filled with people. I thought, "What are they all doing here at midnight?"

Suddenly, I felt like we may be in danger. I told Zane to get in the car. He didn't want to be rude to the boys, so I had to tell him to do it immediately, it was an emergency. He raced over to the passenger side, and slid into the seat as I sped away.

Zane was very bewildered by my actions, but I felt I had been warned, and I sensed that I needed to leave even though I didn't know if I would find gas that night before my tank was empty. Suddenly, staying seemed more risky than running out of gas.

When I arrived in Salt Lake I told a friend about what had happened to me, and he explained that this was the way that some people steal credit. I later read online that "Over the past few years, fraudulent credit card activity has taken the form of gas station scams that use technology to victimize patrons."

"Despite the fact that gas stations have been on thieves' radars for quite some time, many consumers still fail to recognize the tell-tale signs of gas station credit card fraud at the pump."[67]

It was only through the direction of the Spirit and the clear call to *"Look!"* that I was able to be protected from this scheme. It also occurred to me that Heavenly Father often uses this phrase when speaking to His children. I realized that as a parent I unknowingly followed the Lord's example by using the word, "Look" to either direct or protect my family. When I asked my children to "Look," it sometimes was to express my desire that they contemplate the opportunities ahead of them: "Look at that book, or that college, or that audition. Look at the classes you can take, or look at all that you can learn." In 1 Nephi 11:26 "Look!" was the instruction that an angel gave Nephi when he wanted to see the things his father saw. He was caught away to view many glorious visions of the coming events of the world.

"Look!" can also be in the form of a warning. One might say, look out for that dangerous environment, those friends, that situation, or that ideology. Moses was commanded to make a serpent of brass and put it on a pole. Everyone that was bitten by the fiery serpents that were in the land had only to "look" and they would be protected and live (Numbers 21:6-9). Both uses of the word "Look!" can be helpful in our lives.

"Look!" was also the instruction I was given that night and I believe it was in answer to our prayer to have the Lord's watchful care over us as we traveled. Although my view was not glorious in the same way that Nephi's was,

---

[67] Jennifer Calonia, "Ways to Protect Yourself From Credit Card Fraud at Gas Stations," April 9, 2015. http://www.gobankingrates.com/credit-cards/5-tried-true-strategies-protecting-credit-card-gas-pump/

the direction I receive shielded and spared me from being both fleeced and deceived. What a miracle at midnight.

Scrumptious Service

After returning to Texas from living in Guam, I was called as the Relief Society President. Then a physical problem that I thought had gone away, returned. It was a practically crippling pain in my back. I couldn't sit, and I was uncomfortable lying down. I could stand, however, and so during Relief Society I was forced to move to the back of the room where I stood for the entire lesson every Sunday.

I prayed and pleaded for help. I told the Lord I couldn't imagine He wanted me to be in this kind of pain and distress while I was supposed to be serving the sisters. In response to my prayer and not too long after that, I was properly diagnosed and scheduled for back surgery to repair a herniated disc.

The two counselors who served with me in Relief Society were concerned about the needs of my family. They asked if they could bring us a meal after my operation. I wanted to demonstrate one of my core values, which is self-reliance, so I asked them not to bring us anything during my recovery. Besides, at the time, it was just me, my husband, and my high school student. We were very capable of providing our own food. I also hoped to set a good example to others. It was my thought that if it is not an emergency situation, that perhaps preparations could be made ahead of time to take care of a family's needs.

The day after my surgery there was a knock on the door. I had gotten out of bed for a few minutes and so I answered it. It was my two counselors! There they were with warm food and friendly smiles. They had ignored my direction and had come to visit me.

It was the first time I realized that it's not really all about the food. What they brought me was love, and I was so grateful for their friendship, service, and kindness. It also felt like the Lord was watching over me and my family. President Spencer W. Kimball explained one of the methods that Heavenly Father uses to take care of His children: "God does notice us, and he watches over us. But it is usually through another mortal that he meets our needs. Therefore, it is vital that we serve each other in the kingdom."[68]

One of the things that these women knew was that any and all kindnesses are appropriate when guided by the Spirit. This thought is expressed so well in one of my favorite poems:

"I have wept in the night
At my shortness of sight
That to others' needs made me blind,
But I never have yet
Had a twinge of regret
For being a little too kind."
— Anonymous[69]

I never feel uncomfortable about being too kind, whether it is a friendly hello, a generous comment, or a get-real-dirty service. One of the things that has helped me to become a little more proactive in acting upon my "kindness" inspiration came about because I learned the

[68] Spencer W. Kimball, "The Abundant Life," *Ensign,* July 1978.
[69] Anonymous, quoted in Richard L. Evans, "The Quality of Kindness," *Improvement Era,* May 1960, 340.

difference between sins of commission and omission. A sin of commission is to know and understand the commandments, and not to obey them. A sin of omission is to feel that there is something that we can do for someone else, and then decide not to do it. This is how I think the scriptures explain it: "Therefore to him that knoweth to do good, and doeth it not, to him it is sin" (James 4:17). When we feel a tug on our hearts to perform any charitable deed for others, we need to try to act on that prompting.

Sister Linda K. Burton, General Relief Society President, encouraged us to: "First observe, then serve."[70] I believe that she is suggesting that we take the blinders off our eyes and look around us to observe the needs of others. Next, we need to do something about what we see.

These two Relief Society sisters reminded me of another principle President Hinckley expressed: "There is no end to the good we can do, to the influence we can have with others. Let us not dwell on the critical or the negative. Let us pray for strength; let us pray for capacity and desire to assist others. Let us radiate the light of the gospel at all times and all places, that the Spirit of the Redeemer may radiate from us."[71]

The food was delicious, but the kindness was what really filled me. We can be like the Savior who is everlastingly kind as we read in Isaiah, "For the mountains shall depart, and the hills be removed; but my kindness shall not depart from thee" (Isaiah 54:10).

---

[70] Linda K. Burton, "First Observe, Then Serve," *Ensign,* November 2012.

[71] Gordon B. Hinckley, "The Need for Greater Kindness," *Ensign,* May 2006.

Many faithful women truly demonstrated the Relief Society theme that "Charity Never Faileth" through their service and sisterhood. Sister Bonnie L. Oscarson, General Young Women President, expresses the ideal that we could all strive for in our lives: "To be sisters implies that there is an unbreakable bond between us. Sisters take care of each other, watch out for each other, comfort each other, and are there for each other through thick and thin. The Lord has said, 'I say unto you, be one; and if ye are not one ye are not mine.' "[72]

The two thoughtful ladies that labored with me in Relief Society fed me both body and soul. It was truly *scrumptious service*.

---

[72] Bonnie Oscarson, "Sisterhood: Oh, How We Need Each Other," *Ensign*, May 2014.

The True Vine

It has been one of my personal goals to make sure that I am never too busy to serve others. But I am a very goal-oriented person and constantly working on what I want to accomplish. If it wasn't for the Savior's church and the way it is organized, I wonder if I would ever look up from what I am doing to serve those around me. I am spurred on by this meaningful scripture in Mosiah 2:17: "When ye are in the service of your fellow beings ye are only in the service of your God."

The opportunity to serve creates a constant expression of true gratitude in my life. Service seems to me to be the core of growth and goodness in the Church of Jesus Christ of Latter-day Saints. It helps me to reach out beyond my own demands and plans.

I always know that no matter where I live, I will be a Visiting Teacher because I find that not only is it an easy and pleasant way to become better acquainted with the women in my ward, but I am able to be close enough to the sisters and their families so that I can serve them if they need my help. I think the organization of the church is a wonder and a miracle.

I know that Visiting Teaching is an inspired program, but it is also another item on the long list of things that women find that they have to do. And then some sisters just need a visit once a month, but others need more; sometimes, much more.

While I had the constant demands of my large family, loads of laundry, shopping, cooking, cleaning, busing, and mothering, I was also a Visiting Teacher to a very needy sister in my ward. What she required often seemed practically beyond my capabilities. However, I kept trying to fulfill my promises to the Relief Society Presidency, to the Lord, and to her.

One day this sister I visited called me and asked if I could help her with something. I was busy as usual but said I would get right back to her. It surprised me when I looked deeply into my cup of charity and it was empty. Not a bit of benevolence there. Oh! I was so disappointed and dismayed.

I wanted to be able to help her, but I just couldn't see how I could possibly do it. So I prayed. I knelt down in the little room next to my bedroom and said, "Heavenly Father, I really want to serve this sister, but I can't. I don't have the energy, or the desire, or the enthusiasm required. What can I do?"

The words "I am the true vine" came clearly into my mind. Then going to the scriptures to read what was actually written there, I found, "Abide in me, and I in you. As the branch cannot bear fruit of itself, except it abide in the vine; no more can ye, except ye abide in me" (John 15:4).

Then the thought came to me that even though I generally surmised that it was by my own energy and strength that all my good deeds were being accomplished, I was actually drawing on Him to do it all.

"Oh, dear!" I thought. "I didn't realize that I wasn't connecting to the true vine here." I was trying to do this task on my own, and I was coming up short. I immediately asked for His help and proceeded to express my gratitude for every circumstance that had made it possible for me to perform any function in my life. In that quick moment, my perspective changed enough to let me help the sister that day.

Elder Bednar explains, "It is likewise through the grace of the Lord that individuals...receive strength and assistance to do good works that they otherwise would not be able to maintain if left to their own means. This grace is an enabling power that allows men and women to lay hold on eternal life and exaltation after they have expended their own best efforts."

"Can we sense the grace and strengthening power of Christ in the testimony of Ammon? 'Yea, I know that I am nothing; as to my strength I am weak; therefore I will not boast of myself, but I will boast of my God, for in his strength I can do all things; yea, behold, many mighty miracles we have wrought in this land, for which we will praise his name forever' (Alma 26:12). Truly, brothers and sisters, in the strength of the Lord we can do and endure and overcome all things."[73]

I realize that the Lord expects me to do many good works without being compelled, but I also need to remember to call on Him for assistance, and then express gratitude for being able to accomplish anything of worth in the world.

---

[73] David A. Bednar, "In the Strength of the Lord," *Ensign,* November 2004.

Clean and Safe

During the early spring while I was still living in southeast Texas, I decided to drive to Utah. I knew the 24-hour drive was going to be difficult to do by myself. I wouldn't have anyone to keep me company or assist with the driving, but I felt like it was important to go at that time, so I began the trip.

The first part of the journey is usually safe enough because Texas may have torrential rainstorms, but it seldom snows. However, as I drove up to the northern part of the state and into New Mexico, I knew the chance of a spring snowstorm would increase. As I came into Amarillo, I encountered some snow, but as I continued traveling west on Interstate 40 the storm strengthened.

Not only was there blowing snow on the road, but there were also many speeding vehicles splashing globs of the slushy white stuff on my car windows. I remember being squeezed between two large semi-trucks with such low visibility that I wondered if I was going to arrive alive.

At some point in the trip, as the light began to fade, I knew that I needed to locate a place to lodge for the night. I hated to stop because I was alone, and I felt more vulnerable getting out of the car and going into a hotel by myself. I decided to start praying. The words to the prayer that came into my mind were "Please bless me to find something that is clean and safe." Although I was nervous about checking into a strange hotel in an unknown area, I don't think I would have asked the Lord for something with those specific requirements without inspiration.

With slick roads, blowing snow, large trucks, an excess of traffic, and then darkness descending upon me, my prayers intensified. I continue to pray the words that had come into my mind: "Please let me find a hotel that is 'clean and safe.' " Finally I knew that I must get off the freeway and try to find a bed for the night. I decided to exit when the next possible opportunity presented itself.

As I merged to the far right to leave the freeway, I saw a hotel positioned near the side of the road with a well-lit marquee advertising that their place was "Clean and Safe." I was absolutely amazed to see those words in bright letters. It felt similar to an event I had read about in the Book of Mormon. The disciples of Jesus were praying: "And it came to pass that when Jesus…came unto his disciples, and behold, they did still continue, without ceasing, to pray unto him; and they did not multiply many words, for it was given unto them what they should pray" (3 Nephi 19:24). The Spirit can truly teach us how to pray and in this case, having the words given to me that exactly matched the marquee was quite a miracle in my mind. It was Heavenly Father's way of telling me where to stop that night.

It was also a direct answer to prayer and so comforting. When Heavenly Father reaches down and answers us so personally, so kindly, and so lovingly, it adds to our large store of evidence that God does hear and answer prayer. As Christians and believers in an Almighty Power that cares and watches over us, our testimony can change from "I hope" to "I know." Such were my feelings that night as I nestled comfortably in my warm bed and thanked my Heavenly Father for always being there for me. He truly is into the details of our lives.

Our prophet, President Monson, testifies, "I never cease to be amazed by how the Lord can motivate and direct the length and breadth of His kingdom and yet have time to provide inspiration concerning one individual...The fact that He can, that He does, is a testimony to me."

"My brothers and sisters, the Lord is in all of our lives. He loves us. He wants to bless us. He wants us to seek His help. As He guides us and directs us and as He hears and answers our prayers...May we be aware of His blessings in our lives."[74]

I can say with complete confidence that I know that Heavenly Father hears and answers prayers. It is the foundation and rock of my relationship with Him.

---

[74] Thomas S. Monson, "Consider the Blessings," *Ensign,* November 2012.

A Real Person

After saying goodbye to my daughter as she returned to college after a weekend at home, I decided I needed to pray about her dating (or lack of) situation. I was beyond frustrated with the position that both she and I felt that the Lord had required of us: to simply wait. I didn't know if it was possible to go on, and I didn't feel that it was reasonable that the Lord wanted her to postpone her dating life any longer. She was in her 20's and attending college.

I was in my bathroom alone and just fell to my knees pleading with the Lord to allow her to get out of limbo. I asked that He would let her find someone she might like, and that she could perhaps start dating. I received a clear answer to that request. It was so comforting.

Interestingly though, the first thought that came into my mind after I received my answer was, "I wish I could hear that from a real person." I sometimes surprise myself with the sudden ideas that pop into my mind, and even occasionally the things I say in prayer. Once I heard about a family that had suffered the loss of their home through a fire. That night I knelt down and thanked the Lord for His protection of our family through his "matchless" power. I hope the Lord has a sense of humor!

After thinking, "I wish I could hear that from a real person," I had an instantaneous and illuminating response. The Lord shared this important announcement with me: "I am a real person!" Considering all I have learned and know about my Father in Heaven, I shouldn't have needed to hear that, but He sweetly reminded me again.

The world is largely ignorant of the fact that we have a real Father in Heaven, but as Latter-day Saints we understand the nature and personality of the Godhood very clearly. This knowledge is obtained through the abundance of scriptures that are available to us, and also our testimony of Joseph Smith's First Vision,

Besides the actual vision of the prophet, we have convincing commentary on the subject. I love this quote by Stephen Richards regarding Joseph Smith: "When Joseph came out of the grove, he had no need to argue for a theory—he knew the facts; God is in form like a man. He has a voice. He speaks. He is considerate and kind. His Son is a like but distinct person. He is obedient to the Father and the mediator between God and man. The presumption of God as a mere essence or principle of power and force in the universe was for all time exploded. The testimony is direct and positive and irrefutable. Many have not believed, but no one has ever had the knowledge to disprove it."[75]

This statement, coupled with a scripture about the Godhead, makes the fact that He truly is a real person irrefutable: "The Father has a body of flesh and bones as tangible as man's; the Son also; but the Holy Ghost has not a body of flesh and bones, but is a personage of Spirit. Were it not so, the Holy Ghost could not dwell in us" (D&C 130:22).

In General Conference President Monson bore this powerful witness "I bear testimony that this work is true, that our Savior lives, and that He guides and directs His Church here upon the earth. I leave with you my witness

---

[75] Stephen L. Richards, *Where Is Wisdom* (Salt Lake City, Utah: Deseret Books Publishing Company, 1955), 31.

and my testimony that God our Eternal Father lives and loves us. He is indeed our Father, and He is personal and real. May we realize how close to us He is willing to come, how far He is willing to go to help us, and how much He loves us."[76]

With all the evidence available to me, I am sure I will never say that again!

---

[76] Thomas S. Monson, "Until We Meet Again," *Ensign,* May 2014.

They Prayed Us Here

For all forty years of our marriage my husband, Gary, expressed a desire to serve another mission. We met in our twenties while we were both serving in the California North Mission. I was not sure I wanted to go again. I never said "No!" but I was reluctant. I didn't want to leave my home, my children, or my grandchildren. I was feeling fairly confident that I would not serve a second mission as I sat down to listen to the October 2011 General Conference. In his opening remarks President Thomas S. Monson said, "And now to you mature brothers and sisters: we need many, many more senior couples. To the faithful couples now serving or who have served in the past, we thank you for your faith and devotion to the gospel of Jesus Christ. You serve willingly and well and accomplish great good."[77] The minute he said that, I had a confirmation from the Spirit that he was speaking to me.

My husband already felt very prepared to go again because of an experience the previous summer as he camped with the Boy Scouts. During the 100-year anniversary of scouting in the USA, the Sam Houston area council held a jamboree, and over 15,000 boys and their leaders attended. Of those, about 3000 were members of the church. These young scouts attended a fireside in which Elder Gifford Nielsen spoke to them. One of the songs they

[77] Thomas S. Monson, "As We Meet Together," *Ensign,* November 2010.

sang that evening was "We'll Bring the World His Truth."[78] The boys and leaders sang these words: "We have been saved for these latter days to build the kingdom in righteous ways. We hear the words our prophet declares, 'Let each who's worthy go forth and share.'" As Gary sang those words, he felt that he had been preserved, given extra years beyond his retirement, to go forth and share the gospel in righteous ways.

Once Gary and I both agreed we needed to go, we decided to request a mission location, which senior missionaries are allowed to do. Since we had been residing in the warm climate of Texas for many years, and because we had lived in Guam, we requested the Micronesia Guam Mission when we sent in our mission papers. We felt fortunate to have this petition granted when we received our call.

Shortly after that, we spoke with our new mission president, Stephen F. Mecham, on the telephone. He had prayed and considered where to send us, and had decided that we would be located on one of the outer islands, the Republic Palau, for the entire 18 months of our service. When I discovered that we were not going to be living on Guam, I was worried. I read some of the information about my new area, and I wasn't sure I could do that kind of mission. I prayed about it and thought about it, but I still couldn't get a confirmation that it was the right place for me to go. I wanted a testimony of the rightness of that call before I had done anything. I know that a testimony always comes "after" we have the trial of our faith. Only then do we receive the witness (Ether 12:6). Since this mission was

---

[78] "We'll Bring the World His Truth," *Children's Songbook*, 172.

already a leap of faith for me, I hardly felt capable of going forward not knowing if this was the place I was supposed to serve.

On the road to receiving that witness, my husband spoke to our stake president, and in the course of the conversation the president said that he felt the people of Palau had "prayed us there." It was comforting at the time and helped me get over several hurdles that were required to actually travel to the island and stay there.

The first Sunday we were in Palau, the ward was playing the DVD for General Conference that we had just heard the week before while we were in Utah. I enjoyed hearing all the talks again. But before the meeting started, the Elder's Quorum President introduced and welcomed us by saying that "They had prayed that we would come." The other senior couple had left weeks before we got there, and the branch was not always sure if there would be enough senior couples available so that someone could be sent to their island.

In the Micronesia Guam Mission, there are many islands scattered around Guam, and senior couples are sent there to assist the people in any and all ways that they can. We learned that no job was too big or too small, as we taught lessons, led the branch choir, worked with the seminary and institute teachers, received callings in the branch, spoke in church and at baptisms, and taught missionary lessons. We spent a great deal of time searching for the many lost sheep that had been baptized over the years but weren't attending. This was more difficult than we expected because the streets don't have names; everything has to be done by longitude and latitude, and by asking people if they know the person for whom we are looking. We also fed the missionaries and performed service once a week.

I gained a testimony of how important senior missionaries really are. I was also continually assured by the Spirit about the worth of the work we had been called to do. I never felt like we were wasting our time or our lives there.

Knowing that our stake president had been inspired, and that there were members of the church in Palau who were praying for us to come, and then actually hearing it, was the witness I needed to be able to feel like I was in the right place. It reminded me of this statement by Alfred Lord Tennyson that: "More things are wrought by prayer than this world dreams of."[79] The strong, but simple faith of the members on Palau and the inspiration of our stake president was a testimony to me that their prayers were heard!

All through my life, the counsel to depend on prayer has been prized above almost any other advice I have received. It has become an integral part of my journey, an anchor, a constant source of strength, and the basis for my knowledge of things divine.

President Benson said, "'Remember that whatever you do or wherever you are, you are never alone' was my father's familiar counsel to me as a boy. Our Heavenly Father is always near. You can reach out and receive His aid through prayer. I have found this counsel to be true. Thank God we can reach out and tap that unseen power, without which no man can do his best."[80]

[79] Alfred Lord Tennyson, *Selected Poems* (London, England: Penguin Classics, 2007), 38.
[80] Ezra Taft Benson, "Prayer," *Ensign*, May 1977.

Sometimes, even now, I am not always sure that my prayers are getting past the ceiling, but then I remember that the people of Palau prayed, and that their petition reached across an ocean and brought my husband and me to their lovely island.

My Favorite Scripture

Shortly after we arrived in Palau for our mission, my husband and I went to the church to attend seminary class and the Young Women and Young Men activity which were held on the same night. The teacher was late, and so the branch president gathered all the students into the large multi-purpose room that served as both chapel and activity center.

He spoke for a few minutes and then had to go with my husband into his office to do some church business. He asked me to take over, and I had absolutely nothing prepared. I wasn't aware that this kind of thing happened all the time, and that being ready to teach needed to be constantly on my agenda.

Before he left, I asked him what he wanted me to do, and he said, "Read your favorite scripture."

"My favorite scripture?" It is Mosiah 2:41 which says, "And moreover, I would desire that ye should consider on the blessed and happy state of those that keep the commandments of God. For behold, they are blessed in all things, both temporal and spiritual; and if they hold out faithful to the end they are received into heaven, that thereby they may dwell with God in a state of never-ending happiness. O remember, remember that these things are true for the Lord God has spoken it."

The problem for me was that I just didn't feel comfortable reading that scripture to them. It didn't seem right for this group. I had been there less than a week, but I had seen the poverty of a third world country, their low income levels, and the scarcity that these members dealt with every day. I wasn't sure that Mosiah 2:41 would be appropriate; I had never doubted this promise before.

Would the gospel really bless them both temporally and spiritually? How was the Lord going to fulfill that promise in such a poor place? I didn't know. So I didn't read that scripture. I found something else and shared a short gospel message about it.

Since that time I have watched and listened to the brethren to strengthen my testimony of this principle. President Henry B. Eyring, speaking in General Conference, reinforced this for me with a powerful message. He said, "Our Heavenly Father wishes to bless His children spiritually and temporally. He understands each of their needs, their pains, and their hopes.[81]

Over the course of the 18 months that I served there, I learned something that I didn't know before. The Lord is able to bless the faithful members who keep their covenants. He increases their spirituality and improves their lives temporally. The testimonies of the active members are very strong and firm. They stand steadfast against incredible odds that might destroy the faith of others. To live the gospel in so many places on this planet, one has to set aside the culture of their country and embrace the culture of the church. It is very difficult to do this. But, when they do, their lives improve. They don't enjoy the kind of prosperity that other members may take for granted every day, but they have close families and make efforts to go to the temple and keep their covenants.

---

[81] Henry B. Eyring, "Is Not This the Fast That I Have Chosen," *Ensign*, May 2015.

The scriptures with their many promises are not just for one particular place in the world or for a few of Heavenly Father's children. They are for everyone. As the Lord hastens His work throughout the world, He is sending out larger numbers of missionaries to carry the message of the gospel. In this way He is able to bless more and more of His children. The Lord has explained that, "For all who will have a blessing at my hands shall abide the law which was appointed for that blessing, and the conditions thereof, as were instituted from before the foundation of the world" (D&C 132:5).

Some of our leaders have taught that as they have traveled the world they have found that those members who pay their tithing and try to obey the commandments, while also taking time for family prayer and family home evening, are more self-sustaining and need less of the church's welfare services to subsist. In other words, they are able to be more physically and spiritually self-reliant.

I was grateful that I was able to gain a stronger testimony of my favorite scripture as I served on the island of Palau. The Lord can and will bless us if we keep His commandments. No matter where we are in the world, or what our particular situation, we can express our love to our Father in Heaven by doing what He has asked, "If ye love me, keep my commandments." The love we show Him will come back to us in untold blessings.

He Remembers Our Prayers

I have spent many hours on my knees praying for the people that I love best in the whole world. I want my family, my children especially, to have all the blessings of eternity. I also want my prayers to be answered NOW, and so I was comforted to read a scripture that taught me that the Lord had heard my prayers, and that He would answer them in His own time and when it was right for everyone involved. In Mormon 5:21 it says, "And also *the Lord will remember the prayers of the righteous*, which have been put up unto him for them." (Italics added by the author.)

I believe that the Lord wanted me to know that my prayers are not forgotten; He remembers them. He has them close to His heart, and I can feel comforted that they have not flown off to some faraway place in space but will all be answered according to His perfect wisdom.

Continuing on in Mormon 5, the Lord says, "Know ye not that ye are in the hands of God? Know ye not that he hath all power, and at his great command the earth shall be rolled together as a scroll (Mormon 5:23)?" What peace and comfort both of these verses bring to me.

When I was younger and a beginning student of the scriptures, most of the verses seemed to be about keeping the commandments and the consequences of not following the Lord. Now, I find that the scriptures are a source of unspeakable solace. I know *they* haven't changed, so something must have happened to me. When I read verses like this one in Isaiah, I am filled with light and hope and comfort: "Can a woman forget her sucking child, that she should not have compassion on the son of her womb? Yea, they may forget, yet will I not forget thee. Behold, I have graven thee upon the palms of my hands; thy walls are continually before me" (Isaiah 49:15-16).

Parents understand this kind of love and caring. Our children are so dear to us that we want to make sure that we nurture them sufficiently. Sometimes we aren't perfect in this endeavor. One of the stories that parents relate to each other is about accidentally leaving their child behind. It happens. Even very conscientious parents have told me of leaving one of their children and the anxiety they felt until they could get back to them.

I remember one Sunday when my husband, Gary, took one car to church and I took another. Then we both drove home separately, and when we got there we discovered that we were one child short of our seven. It was frightening for us, but I know it doesn't happen to our Father in Heaven.

The Lord never loses track of us, what we want, or what we need. It is comforting to know that even though the Lord has created "worlds without number" (Moses 1:33) still "The very hairs of your head are all numbered" to Him (Matthew 10:30).

Enoch understood the Lord's immense capacity to minister to His children when he asks the Lord a question and then proceeded to make a declaration about His personality: "Thou art holy, and from all eternity to all eternity. And were it possible that man could number the particles of the earth, yea, millions of earths like this, it would not be a beginning to the number of thy creations; and thy curtains are stretched out still; and yet thou art there, and thy bosom is there; and also thou art just; thou art merciful and kind forever" (Moses 7:29-30).

If all my desires and prayers are not answered immediately, I still feel safe in the arms of the Lord's love, kindness, and mercy. He remembers forever.

He Is There

Several years ago I had the sweet pleasure of spending over a month with my daughter, Jocelyn, and her three children. We participated in many activities during that time, including going to a family arcade. While she played with the two older children, I decided to follow my 20-month-old grandson, Peter, around. In essence he had free rein to wander wherever he wanted. He loved it.

I walked a few paces behind him, but I never let him out of my sight. I began to notice the astonished looks on the faces of adults when he toddled past them, looking essentially alone. One woman started to leap out of her chair when she saw him. She was immediately intent on protecting him from any danger that he might encounter. Then she saw me and sat back down.

As I quietly accompanied Peter around the play area, an impression began to instill upon my mind. The thought was, "He doesn't even know I am here." I was watching over him, protecting him, and providing for his every need from moment to moment, but he didn't know it.
Then this sprang into my mind: "That's how I care for you." The Lord wanted me to know that I am His little child, and even though I don't always realize, notice, or remember it, He is always there, protecting, guiding, and watching over me. This message was actually delivered twice that summer, and I understand now that I am never out of His sight.

I am grateful that the leaders of the church are always reminding me of my Father in Heaven's constant care and watchful nature, but I never had a personal witness of it until this happened. One of the many statements regarding the Lord's personal attention came from President Hinckley who shared his thoughts in this way, "The Almighty is blessing his church and his people. He is watching over them. He neither slumbers nor sleeps as he guides, directs, and moves in his own 'mysterious way His wonders to perform' " (Hymns, no. 48).[82]

It is difficult to comprehend that our Father in Heaven can have such a personal interest and concern for each of us. The Lord is not only following quietly behind us, but He is actively participating in our lives. As Elder Bednar reminds us, "The Lord's tender mercies are the very personal and individualized blessings, strength, protection, assurances, guidance, loving-kindnesses, consolation, support, and spiritual gifts which we receive from and because of and through the Lord Jesus Christ."[83]

When I reflect back upon my life-long quest to come to know the Lord through prayer, scripture study, service, and commitment to His cause, I am grateful for the testimony that I have been given that the Lord is always there. We are never alone no matter how we may sometimes feel.

I love to have the words of Sister DeFord's song come floating into my mind at various times during the day, and then I will find myself singing these comforting words:

[82] Gordon B. Hinckley, "He Slumbers Not, nor Sleeps," *Ensign,* May 1983.
[83] David A. Bednar, "What Are the Tender Mercies of the Lord?" *Ensign*, May 2005.

He is there with love beyond our understanding
Watching o'er us with a Father's tender care
With all His might and mercy never-ending
He is there[84]

Truly, He is there!

---

[84] See Sally DeFord, "He Is There,"
http://www.defordmusic.com/sheet-music/alphabetical-list/he-is-there/

Share your Miraculous Moments
with others in my second volume,
My Miraculous Moments, Too

Email your story to:
gailhjohnsen@gmail.com

To schedule Gail as a speaker,
for comments or questions,
contact the email address above.

34610526R00093

Made in the USA
San Bernardino, CA
02 June 2016